Empedocles

Empedocles

HELLE LAMBRIDIS

with a prefatory essay
EMPEDOCLES AND T. S. ELIOT
by Marshall McLuhan

Studies in the Humanities No. 15
Philosophy

THE UNIVERSITY OF ALABAMA PRESS
University, Alabama

CONTENTS

Empedocles and T. S. Eliot
(by Marshall McLuhan)   vi
Abbreviations of Works Cited   xvi
1. Sources   1
2. Life and Legend   7
3. Contemporaries   22
4. Physics and Metaphysics   40
5. Sensation and Knowledge   73
6. Biology   92
7. Cosmology   106
8. Conversion   116
9. Poetry   136
Index   146

EMPEDOCLES AND T. S. ELIOT
Marshall McLuhan

The vision of Empedocles may have made its *entrée* into English literature via Lewis Carroll rather than Matthew Arnold, in the image of Humpty Dumpty (the *Sphairos*) rather than the haggard suicide of Mount Aetna (*Empedocles on Aetna*). Lewis Carroll, the non-Euclidean geometer, was a more suitable person than Her Majesty's Superintendant of Schools to bring Empedocles and the *Sphairos* to the British public. The playful mathematician was better qualified than the Victorian moralist to bring the space-time vision of Empedocles to English literature and to the rocking-horse world of the nursery. The nursery world of myth and mutations was where Empedocles first established a major beach-head in the Victorian age.

It is when Alice has gone through the Looking-Glass that she encounters Humpty Dumpty "with his legs crossed like a Turk, on the top of a high wall—such a narrow one that Alice quite wondered how he could keep his balance." At once they plunge into the world of words and names and the magical transformations inseparable from language. Carroll, whose own name, Dodgson, is full of puns, took the pen name of Lewis Carroll, which involved him immortally in the acoustic world of song and resonance. He is able to speak from both sides in the Looking-Glass at once, even as Empedocles does in the words of Dr. Lambridis: His phrase "I shall speak a double truth," repeated again and again . . . means that Love, which unites the elements in due proportion and produces such varied forms of life, also destroys them; and Strife, which

creates monsters and havoc, also makes a beginning in the formation of live creatures, but again destroys them before the *Sphairos*
returns to wipe out all differences. Hence: "Double is the birth of
mortal things and double their demise."

"Must a name mean something?" Alice asked doubtfully.

"Of course it must," Humpty Dumpty said with a short laugh:
my name means the shape I am. . . . With a name like yours, you
might be any shape almost."

Carroll is having some rather profound fun, for Alice is the Greek
sound for *alas*, which is salt. And salt as sign of life and preserva-
tion is put on the tongue of the infant in Catholic baptism when
the name is given. So, Humpty Dumpty rightly says: "With a
name like yours, you might be any shape, almost."

There is another aspect to the doubleness of the traditional
Humpty Dumpty verses which emerges when they are given a
phonetic translation into French:

Un petit d'un petit
S'étonne aux Halles
Un petit d'un petit
Ah! degrés fallent.

Indolent qui ne sort cesse
Indolent qui ne se mène
Q'importe un petit d'un petit
Tout Gai de Requennes.
       Mots D'Heures Gousses Rames
        Luis d'Antin Van Rooten

Read aloud, these verses are transformed into English, as in the
whole of *Finnegans Wake* by James Joyce, who said of it: "What
the reader sees will not be what he hears." It is quite fitting therefore, that Alice and Humpty Dumpty should discuss words, since,
as the very informing principle of cosmic action, it is language itself that embodies and performs the dance of being. Humpty
Dumpty, the cosmic egg, says: "I can explain all the poems that

ever were invented—and a good many that haven't been invented just yet."

This remark by Humpty Dumpty invites a look at the work of T. S. Eliot, whose essay on "Tradition and the Individual Talent" explains that a traditional writer will have the historical sense ". . . and the historical sense involves a perception, not only of the pastness of the past, but of its presence; the historical sense compels a man to write not merely with his own generation in his bones, but with a feeling that the whole of the literature of Europe from Homer and within it the whole of the literature of his own Country has a simultaneous existence and composes a simultaneous order." Dr. Lambridis brings out this quality of the nourishment of the individual talent by traditional or corporate awareness, in Empedocles (page 85):

> But if thou adherest to these things steadfastly in thy strong mind, considering them with good intent and selfless pure study, they'll all be with thee throughout thy life in high degree, and thou wilt have acquired much else from them; for they by themselves increased in stature, in the direction of each one's nature."

Having studied Eliot for decades, but having only recently been introduced to Empedocles by Dr. Lambridis, I can say that my sense of the bearings and significance not only of Homer but of the work of Eliot and his contemporaries has been changed and deepened.

T. S. Eliot spent his life in philosophical as well as poetic endeavors, having had long training at Harvard, and in France and Germany, in the thought of East and West. His devotion to the pre-Socratic philosophers is evident in his citation from them, but it is Empedocles whose vision pervades *The Waste Land* and *Four Quartets*. Eliot was not alone in his recourse to Empedocles. It would be quite easy to show how deeply W. B. Yeats and Ezra Pound and James Joyce had also studied Empedocles. Many of their most memorable figures and images are central to the work of Empedocles, and perhaps the reason is to be found in a single phrase of T.S. Eliot, "*the auditory imagination.*" The process to which this phrase refers is central to all the great poets of the West from Poe to Valéry.

The visual imagination had insulated the poets from many of their traditional resources for several ages. The acoustic space created by the simultaneous information environment, from the telegraph on, related men and societies in a new world of resonant interface. The visual separations and definitions, of words and peoples alike, could no longer hold. Freud's breakthrough into the "unconscious" was a recognition that private consciousness was created by the suppression of corporate awareness. Eliot transferred this awareness to language:

> What I call the "auditory imagination" is the feeling for syllable and rhythm, penetrating far below the conscious levels of thought and feeling, invigorating every word: sinking to the most primitive and forgotten, returning to the origin and bringing something back, seeking the beginning and the end. It works through meanings, certainly, or not without meanings in the ordinary sense, and fuses the old and obliterated, and the trite, the current, and the new and the surprising, the most ancient and the most civilized mentality.

The "auditory imagination" is a norm in Empedocles and is the reason why the merely visual imagination of Aristotle, the classifier, could not apprehend Empedocles. It is only now in the electric age, when both Greek and Newtonian "Nature" can be seen as merely visual systems of classification, that the "Nature" of Empedocles resumes its relevance.

W.B. Yeats concludes his poem "Among School Children" with a meditation that is not only typical of Yeats but Empedocles:

> O body swayed to music, O brightening glance,
> How can we know the dancer from the dance?

Even more congenial to Empedocles is the Yeats idea of "The Emotion of Multitude" or universality:

> The Shakespearian drama gets the emotion of multitude out of the sub-plot which copies the main plot, much as a shadow upon

the wall copies one's body in the firelight. We think of *King Lear* less as the history of one man and his sorrows than as the history of a whole evil time. Lear's shadow is in Gloucester, who also has ungrateful children, and the mind goes on imagining other shadows, shadow beyond shadow, till it has pictured the world.

A sense of universality is magically evoked by this parallel without connections:

> In *Hamlet,* one hardly notices, so subtly is the web woven, that the murder of Hamlet's father and the sorrow of Hamlet are shadowed in the lives of Fortinbras and Ophelia and Laertes, whose fathers, too, have been killed. It is so in all the plays, or in all but all, and very commonly the sub-plot is the main plot working itself out in more ordinary men and women, and so doubly calling up before us the image of multitude.

The reader of *The Waste Land* encounters a musical structure of Love and Strife celebrating life-in-death and death-in-life:

> April is the cruellest month, breeding
> Lilacs out of the dead land, mixing
> Memory and desire

Dr. Lambridis cites the biological theory of Empedocles as "a primitive forestalling of Darwin's theory of evolution," but the reader of *Four Quartets* will find a fulfilment of Empedocles' cosmology ever more satisfying. Each of the four parts of this poem is assigned to celebrate one of the four elements:

> Burnt Norton (air)
> East Coker (earth)
> Dry Salvages (water)
> Little Gidding (fire)

Each poem also celebrates a specific place, for,

> If all time is eternally present
> All time is unredeemable.

It is the space-time of the particularized intersection of a space and a time that transforms and purifies:

> To be conscious is not to be in time
> But only in time can the moment in the rose-garden . . .
> Be remembered; involved with past and future.

Re-membering, re-structuring, the re-cognition, the re-tracing of the labyrinth of perception is central to the mode of Empedocles:

> I shall now retrace my step and come back to my song's beginning.

This is the opening of the second Quartet, *East Coker*:

> In my beginning is my end.

This motto of Mary Queen of Scots proclaims Love as the final cause or pattern. But the process itself manifests more of Strife than love, as in the first Quartet *Burnt Norton*:

> Garlic and sapphires in the mud
> Clot the bedded axle-tree.
> The trilling wire in the blood
> Sings below inveterate scars
> And reconciles forgotten wars.

History is made by time as time is made by meaning, and the meaning is revealed by the replay or the retracing of an experience. Thus, *Four Quartets* is "a series of images of migration" by which the circulating life of man is enclosed and held in place.

> And so we moved, and they, in a formal pattern,
> Along the empty alley, into the box circle,
> To look down into the empty pool.

"The box circle" is a witty arrest of the *Sphairos* between the complementary modes of vegetation and wooden artifact, between the outer garden and the inner theatre. The arrested music of the *Sphairos* is caught again at the end of *Burnt Norton*:

> Only by the form, the pattern
> can words or music reach
> the stillness, as a Chinese jar still
> moves perpetually in its stillness

Eliot has placed the sayings of Heraclitus at the beginning of
Burnt Norton: Although the Law of Reason (*logos*) is common,
the majority of people live as though they had an understanding
(wisdom) of their own. The ways upward and downward are the
same. Both of these are spoken from the world of acoustic space in
which there is no private identity, nor any upside-down. Yet they
sound paradoxical to a literate or visually oriented person. Nobody
could have been more literate than Eliot, and yet nobody could
have had more empathy for the non-visual world of the preliter-
ate. Probably, by comparison with the intense literacy of the
print-accustomed man, Empedocles and his contemporaries would
have seemed to us to be men of oral rather than literate culture,
able to move easily across cultural boundaries by resonant sym-
pathy, recognizing that opposites are complementary aspects of
the same thing. The sayings of Heraclitus provide *Four Quartets*
with themes relevant to both Christian and Hindu thought, and
the verses of Empedocles which Dr. Lambridis presents on page
68 seem almost to have been embodied in *Four Quartets*:

> I shall speak a double truth; at times
> one alone comes into being;
> at other times out of one several things grow.
> Double is the birth of mortal things and double their demise.
> For the coming together of all both causes their birth
> and destroys them; and separation nurtured in their
> being makes them fly apart. These things never stop
> changing throughout, at times coming together through
> Amity in one whole, at other times being violently
> separated by Strife. Thus, on one side, one whole
> is formed out of many, and then again, wrenched from
> each other, they make up many out of one. This is
> the way they become, and their life is not long their
> own, but in as far as they never stop changing throughout
> in so far they are always immobile in a circle.
> But come, listen to my words; for knowledge makes
> the mind grow.
>
> As I said once before, revealing the outer limits of my
> thought, I shall tell a double truth: At times one alone
> grows out of many, at other times they grow apart, the

many out of the one. Fire and water and earth and the
immeasurable height of air, and, away from them all, the
awful Strife all over. Amity among them, equal on all
sides in length and breadth. Look thou at her, don't
sit there astounded by sight. Amity is believed by
men to be innate in their bones. . . .

Each of the Empedocles passages stresses "a double truth." This is
a matter central to Eliot, but it is also closely involved in the work
of Yeats, who, as I have suggested, has elucidated the procedure in
his brief essay on "The Emotion of Multitude." This emotion, or
sense of the universal in the particular, is born of "a double truth,"
somewhat in the mode of Quantum Mechanics where the chemical
bond is the result not of a connection but of a "resonant interval"
such as must obtain between the wheel and the axle. The means
indicated by Yeats for achieving the emotion of multitude are
familiar to modern students of Shakespeare under the head of
"double plots," and these means were taught in antiquity as essential to the aitiological epic or the Epyllion. (See Marjorie Crump's
The Epyllion from Theocritus to Ovid.)

Paradoxically the sudden intrusion of Empedocles in the midst
of his account of the cosmic process has exactly the effect that
Yeats describes in "The Emotion of Multitude." The sudden encounter between the author and his readers, or between the author
and his medium (language), creates an unexpected involvement in
the very making process itself. As Dr. Lambridis says on page 86:

> Empedocles feels keenly that what he has to say about the higher
> level is inconceivable and almost impossible to express by the
> available linguistic means. . . . As far as I know, he is the only
> philosopher (pre- or post-Socratic) to have acknowledged him-
> self baffled by the gap between what he has conceived and what
> it is possible to express adequately."

The gap was never more strikingly indicated than by Baudelaire
in his envoi: *hypocrite lecteur mon semblable, mon frère;* or by
Dostoevsky in *Notes from Underground*:

I write only for myself, and I wish to declare once and for all that if I write as though I were addressing readers, that is simply because it is easier for me to write only in that form. It is a form, an empty form—I shall never have readers.

It is precisely this gap that has, paradoxically, afforded Eliot some of his most effective expression in *Four Quartets*. Where Empedocles says self-deprecatingly: "I too talk like that by force of usage," Eliot says in *East Coker*:

That was a way of putting it—not very satisfactory: A periphrastic study in a worn-out poetical fashion. . . .

But the big moment comes in *Little Gidding*, the last quartet when Eliot confronts *il miglior fabbro* as in another world:

So I assumed a double part, and cried
And heard another's voice cry: 'What! are *you* here?'
Knowing myself yet being someone other.

Not only is there the dramatic play between Eliot and Pound but between themselves and their medium:

Since our concern was speech, and speech impelled us
To purify the dialect of the tribe
And urge the mind to aftersight and foresight. . . .

Here, as everywhere in Empedocles, there is concern with the need and means for purification. It is the common measure, speech itself, the agent of perception that is the prime responsibility of the poets; for, as Dr. Lambridis explains (p. 87), in Empedocles there is no direct way to the higher levels:

The wise man must try to join the peaks of thought by many different ways. He must experiment in his mind . . . and mould the pieces together with 'pure intent'.

Immediately after the words quoted above from Eliot, he gives an eloquent inventory of "the gifts reserved for age" in a way that recalls his earlier *Gerontion*. In *Gerontion* too there is a dramatic dissolution and retrieval of the four elements, he is a kind of *Sphairos* or Humpty Dumpty "driven by the Trades." Everywhere, Eliot is concerned with what Dr. Lambridis calls the spiritualization of the *Sphairos*:

> With great diffidence I venture to suggest that the conception of the spiritualisation of the Sphairos . . . may be due to a more remote influence: that of Buddhism. (p. 120)

Eliot is deeply aware of this great current, but also urges attention to the perversity of Adam, the "ruined millionaire." Adam, too, is a *Sphairos* in *Four Quartets* and "the ultimate cure of rebirth depends upon the wounded surgeon, Christ, who plies the steel and the dying nurse, the Church, that reminds us that the agony of dying is necessary to rebirth." (See Geo. Williamson *A Reader's Guide to T. S. Eliot*, N. Y. Noonday Press, 1953, p. 221)

ABBREVIATIONS OF WORKS CITED

AA	Aristotle. *De Anima*
AC	_____. *De Caelo*
APA	_____. *De Partibus Animalium*
ADP	_____. *De Poetis* (Fragmenta)
ADR	_____. *De Respiratione*
ADS	_____. *De Sensu*
AGC	_____. *De Generatione et Corruptione*
AMP	_____. *Metaphysica*
AML	_____. *Meteorologica*
AP	_____. *Poetica*
AR	_____. *Rhetorica*
ASE	_____. *Sophistici Elenchi*
BE	E. Bignone. *Empedocle* (Turin, 1916; reprinted 1963).
CMG	*Corpus Medicorum Graecorum*, 1908–; Leipzig, Berlin, B. G. Teubner (pre-war); Berlin, Akademie Verlag (post-war).
CW	C. Wachsmuth. *Ioannis Stobaeus* (Berlin, 1884).
DK	*Die Fragmente der Vorsokratiker*, ed. and tr. H. Diels, sixth edition, revised by Walther Kranz, (Dublin/Zurich: Wiedemann, 1952).
	Dr. Lambridis follows Diels in the numbering of the fragments.
DL	Diogenes Laertius. *History of Philosophers.*
DCV	Dionysius the Thracian. *De Compositione Verborum.*
DOX	*Doxographi Graeci*, ed. H. Diels, Berlin, 1879.
FGH	*Fragmente der Griechischen Historiker*, ed. F. Jacoby, 1923-58 (Berlin, Weidmann, 1923-30; Leiden, E. J. Brill, 1940-58).
FHG	*Fragmenta Historicum Graecum*, ed. C. Miller (Paris, 1874).
HE	Herodotus
NP	A. Nauck, *Porphyrii Philosophi Platonici* (Leipzig, 1886)
PF	Plutarch. *De Fortuna Alexandri*
PP	_____. *Pericles*
POL	_____. *De facie in orbe lunae*
PQC	_____. *Quaestiones Conviviales*
PQR	_____. *Quaestiones Romanae*
VH	O. Voss. *De Heraclides Pontici: vita et scriptis* (Rostock, 1896).
WS	Wilamowitz. *Sitzungsberichte der Berliner Akademie der Wissenschaften* (1929).

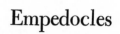

Empedocles

1. THE SOURCES

The standard books on the history of ancient Greek philosophy, with a few notable exceptions, deal with Empedocles briefly and almost contemptuously in a few pages. He is usually considered a "pluralist" along with Anaxagoras, to whom he bears but a very remote resemblance. Even those who have studied his theory of the "mixture" have almost always misunderstood the stages of that mixture's process. For instance, a lengthy study by Ettore Bignone, first published in 1916 and reprinted without additions or amendments in 1963, though unsurpassed in detailed knowledge of the Empedoclean fragments, is vitiated by its intent to show that Empedocles was a mystic from the outset.

Empedocles is a very important philosopher who made an original synthesis of the theories current in his time, who combined intellectual excitement and passion with a high degree of intellectual effort, and who, moreover, can be called the greatest philosopher-poet of the ancient world. These two attributes—poetry and philosophy—have for long been considered incompatible. Certain men of letters inspired by the poetry of Empedocles' fragments (Hölderlin, Romain Rolland, and Matthew Arnold) were scarcely competent to deal with the philosophic content of his work. On the other hand, the professional philosophers have disregarded his poetry almost completely. I have tried to bridge these critical inadequacies and, further, to give an intelligible form to some admittedly difficult and puzzling passages in his work.

It is almost entirely due to Empedocles' poetic imagination and

1

force of expression that a considerable part of his work has been preserved, albeit in fragments. According to some scholars, these fragments amount to one-tenth of his total work; according to others, one-sixth. This is more than has been preserved of the work of any other pre-Socratic philosopher.

Source material regarding Empedocles' life extends over more than eight hundred years. Practically all the ancient commentators included references to his work—chiefly in the form of passing allusions or derogatory remarks. Aristotle mentioned Empedocles in his *De Anima, De Caelo, De Generatione et Corruptione, Metaphysica, Poetica, Rhetorica, Sophistici Elenchi,* and (fragmentary) *De Poetis.* Theophrastus, of the Aristotelian school (4th-3rd cent. B.C.), is one of the most reliable sources of information about Empedocles, in his *Meteorologica,* his *De Respiratione,* and especially in his treatise *De Sensu,* which deals with the philosopher's theory of sensation. Although inevitably influenced by Aristotle, Theophrastus makes quite clear what it is that he is combating.

Another important source stems from the end of the eight-hundred year period during which pre-Socratic philosophy was thought worthy of time and trouble. Diogenes Laertius, in the 4th century A.D., wrote a *History of Philosophers* in ten books. Nothing is known about Diogenes Laertius himself, not even his real name. Diogenes Laertius is a pen name, a twisted version of the customary way of addressing Odysseus in Homer's *Odyssey:* "Divine born son of Laertes." He did a remarkable work of collation, although he quoted his sources without chapter or verse. Not being a philosopher himself, he had no bias for or against one philosopher or another. In the eighth book of his *History,* he devoted thirty chapters to Empedocles. He also referred to Empedocles in other books of the *History,* when writing of other thinkers; but though he provided a genealogical tree, so to say, showing the origins and the succession of all schools of philosophic thought, he did not consider Empedocles an originator of any of them.

To return to the earlier commentators: There was a considerable time gap between Theophrastus and the other scholiasts. It covered the period when the Stoic and Epicurean schools of philosophy were flourishing as well as the Cynics and the other off-shoots of the Socratic teachings, and when those of a philosophical bent committed themselves to one or another of these schools of thought. It was only during the centuries immediately before and after Christ that commentators and historians of philosophy began to multiply. This was a time when all writers apparently thought themselves capable of authoritative opinions on all philosophical matters. Their statements must be taken with reserve, especially those of the Christian converts, and of others definitely committed to specific schools of philosophy; and reserve must also be extended to those who based themselves on Platonic or Aristotelian conceptions. Further, the writing of *vies romancées* of the ancient philosophers was in full swing by the early Christian centuries.

Sextus Empiricus, one of the earliest commentators, flourished during the middle of the second century B.C. The title of his main work *Adversus Mathematicos* is misleading. He did not in fact attack the mathematicians, but the "mathemata"; that is, the forerunner of the medieval quadrivium, consisting of the humanist studies of grammar, rhetoric, logic, and dialectics. Sextus Empiricus was fundamentally a sceptic; he did not believe in these mental disciplines and thought their proofs amounted to very little.

Various writers of the early Christian centuries used Alexander the Knowledgable, of the first century B.C., as a major source of reference. He seems to have been more positive than many.

The more factual writers include Aëtius, of the second century A.D., who wrote *On What Philosophers Like* and a *Collection of Physical Opinions*; Aelianos (Claudius), nickname for the Sophist who lived probably in the first half of the third century A.D. and who wrote *On the Qualities of Animate Beings* and *Varied History;* and Hierocles, who belonged to the Alexandrian branch of the Neoplatonic school of the fifth century A.D. and who wrote a commentary on the *Golden Sayings of Pythagoras* (a book that was anything but authentic) and *On the Making of the World,* as well as books on the Neoplatonic Proclus and others.

The Christian theologian Philoponos (John) tried, like others before and after him, to find the root of the Christian religion in the disconnected sayings of the ancient philosophers, and sometimes touched on logical questions. With him must be ranged Clemens of Alexandria, who lived between (probably) 150 and 216 A.D. His best-known work, *Stromateis*, deals with several of the Greek philosophers and is more reliable than most, though greatly biassed by his newly acquired Christianity. The writings of Favorinus of the first half of the third century A.D. include his *History of All Sorts*, a rich but unreliable source of information.

Contemporary with the early Christian scholiasts, several of the pagan Neoplatonists have left useful comments on Empedocles. Porphyry, from Phoenicia to Tyre, the immediate successor of Plotinus, wrote abundantly on the pre-Socratic philosophers, besides organizing the works of his master in the famous Enneads, each containing nine treatises. His commentary on Plato's *Timaeus* endeavored to show the inner connection of Plotinus with Plato; and Porphyry's passing references to pre-Socratic philosophers are serious and worth considering, despite his mystical bias. One of his works is interestingly titled *On the Starting-points which lead us to the Intelligible*. He also wrote a *History of the Philosophers* and a *vie romancée* of Pythagoras. Porphyry's life covered the last three quarters of the third century A.D. Proclus, another Neoplatonist, belonged to the Athenian branch of the school. He is important upon his own subject, as he had thoroughly studied the logical treatises of Aristotle and the Stoics. He is biassed. Like so many others of his time (fifth century A.D.), he entitled one of his works *On Providence*, not disregarding the difficult questions arising from his subject. Synesius, approximately 370-413 A.D., also wrote a treatise titled *On Providence*. He came from the Greek mainland, and he had been influenced to some degree by the teaching of the Stoa. He left a great many Epistles, supposedly 159 in total. Yet another Neoplatonist, Simplicius, of the fifth century A.D., assembled collections of essays written by earlier philosophers. It is probably he who coined the word *anthology*. He wrote much about Empedocles, though rather superficially. The Neoplatonist Iamblichus was one of the few who concerned himself with the problems raised by arithmetic. He lived to nearly 330 A.D., by which year we know from various sources that he was certainly dead. All the Neoplatonists were far more interested in the second work of Empedocles, the *Purifications*, than in his first work, *On Nature*. They read into the *Purifications* parts of the myths of Plato about the soul and its immortality, and about the soul shedding its wings, after which it is forced to return to the earthly life; but there is no mention of wings in any of the extant fragments of Empedocles.

In mentioning sources, we cannot omit Plutarch, the Theban (50-125 A.D.), whose ambition was to be a universal mind. His best-known work is the *Parallel Lives of Greek and Roman Statesmen and Generals*. One wishes he had written parallel lives of the philosophers, but he had hardly enough material on the Roman side to attempt anything like that. He also wrote a great many treatises on the most varied subjects, including *On Osiris and Isis, Quaestiones Conviviales, On the Face in the Lunar Circle, Quaestiones Naturales, On the Pythian Oracle*, etc. He mentions Empedocles in many of his works and we are indebted to him for preserving a sentence of Empedocles' own about the moon, to which no other extant fragment corresponds.

Further sources of information include Neanthes (240-150 B.C.); the historian Satyros, who lived in Egypt during the reign of Ptolemy VI; and a little later, in the second century B.C., Dionysius the Thracian, who though born in Alexandria, appended Thrace to his name because his father came from there. Both Neanthes and Satyros wrote treatises *On Famous Men*, and engaged in a lively controversy with each other. The very learned Dionysius taught in Rhodes, then an important intellectual center. He was one of the first to teach literary criticism in its contemporary sense. His *The Art of Grammar*, which has been preserved, gave rise to many comments among the Byzantine scholars, notably Stephanos the Byzantine. It was published in Europe in the eighteenth century.

Finally, two modern collections contain fragmentary bits of information on, and quotations from, the ancient philosophers: the *Fragmenta Historicum Graecum* and *Die Fragmente der Griechischen Historiker*. The important collection by H. Diels of the Doxographers (*Doxographi Graeci*) contains much interesting material. The Doxographi were teachers who composed anthologies of famous sayings; they transmitted some of the fragments of Empedocles. However, their comments can be disregarded with an easy conscience.

Though his nearest and greatest successors—Plato, Aristotle, and Theophrastus—often refer to Empedocles (as will be noted in detail later), the first and the third completely ignore all details relating to his life, while Aristotle cursorily intersperses some data here and there. All other information regarding Empedocles' life stems from much later sources: some from the Alexandrian commentators, and some from the early Christian, each writer culling from his forebears. Their writings preserved genuine passages of Empedoclean philosophy. These passages jump out, so to say, from the platitudes of scholiasts because the language of Empedocles is older and more original than the commentary. The criterion of the genuine character of such fragments is the language employed. The compilers could not imitate the pure Ionian of Heraclitus or the rich language of Empedocles, studded with local words, or words invented by him; hence such characteristics stamp their sayings as authentic. The genuineness of the Empedoclean texts is thus pretty well assured. The same is true for the scanty fragments of Heraclitus and Parmenides—the latter because he wrote in verse (though unpoetical) and the former because of his highly original methods of expression, which could scarcely be imitated by commentators. On the other hand, Anaxagoras, who wrote in the already developed Attic tongue, may often have been misquoted or paraphrased.

2. LIFE AND LEGEND

Just as the life of Goethe consisted, in his own words, of poetry and truth (*Dichtung und Wahrheit*), so traditions of the life of Empedocles are a medley of fact and fantasy.

Empedocles' City. Empedocles was born in Akragas sometime during the Olympiad 496–493 B.C. Akragas was a flourishing Greek colony on the south shore of Sicily, on a ridge above the river from which it got its name. It was founded in 581 B.C. and was actually a colony of the colony of Gela, which lay some distance to the east. Gela, established just over a hundred years previously, had been founded by two men, a Cretan and a Rhodian. This is rather rare in the history of Greek colonization. Usually a single city sent out a party of colons under the leadership of one man, and the resulting colony owed allegiance to the mother-city (the metropolis), sending delegations with gifts to its yearly festivals, and consulting it on matters of foreign policy. We have no reports of such relations between Gela and either Crete or Rhodes. The life of the city of Akragas extended over a little less than two centuries. Established at the beginning of the sixth century B.C., it was besieged by the Carthaginians in 404 B.C. Its inhabitants, reduced by famine, were allowed to leave it with whatever of their belongings they could carry. Much later, the city was repopulated under the Romans and renamed Agrigenthum.

During the two centuries of its existence as a Greek colony, Akragas rose to prosperity and civic independence. It contained at least six Doric temples, one of them the second largest in the Greek world. Empedocles noting the luxurious way of life of his fellow citizens, is reported to have said: "The Akragantines feast as if they were going to die tomorrow, and build their houses as if they were going to live forever." That he loved his city dearly is attested by the opening lines of the first fragment of his *Purifications*, in which, addressing his friends, he says:

> Oh, my friends, who inhabit the great city on the banks of fair Akragas, on the high part of the city, mindful of good works, harboring the strangers whom you honor, inexperienced in evil deeds, Hail!

Now Gela, and therefore also Akragas, were "given," in the expression of Thucydides (VI, IV, 4), Doric institutions and customs. Hence, officially and technically, Akragas was a Dorian city and Empedocles a Dorian. Yet there are signs, which will be more fully developed when we examine his work, that both Empedocles and his city deviated from the usual type of Doric policy and behavior. For instance, Akragas lay between Gela on the east and Selinus on the west; yet, when both these cities sided with the Syracusans against the Athenian invasion, 415–413 B.C., Akragas managed to remain neutral and refused to permit the Lacedemonian general, Gylippos, to cross its territory (Thucydides, VII, xxxii, 1). Also, Akragas twice experienced a sudden change of regime, unlike other Dorian cities. The first time, Empedocles was instrumental in overthrowing the rule of "the Thousand"; on the second occasion, their immediate descendants recaptured power and exiled Empedocles.

Empedocles is reported by Aristotle (ADP fr. 70) to have composed an epic on Xerxes' attack on Greece in 480 B.C. If this was so, Empedocles must have been the only Sikeliot to have taken notice of that world-shaping event.

Finally, the islands of Crete and Rhodes, whence came the colonists of Gela, Akragas' mother-city, had been great and populous centers of the pre-Greek, Aegean civilization long before their conquest by the Dorians. Memories of previous high levels of culture die hard; it is very probable that Empedocles not only preserved many of the elements of that earlier culture, but that he considered it as marking the high point of peace and prosperity for mankind.

In any case, we can assume that Akragas was inhabited by people of mixed descent—Dorians, Achaeans, and perhaps Aegeans —and that it was free from the usual Dorian prejudices. It is difficult to judge the size of the city of Akragas. Heraclides gives the number of its inhabitants as 800,000, which is manifestly too great (VH, fr. 72). Wilamowitz, contesting this, reduces the population to 20,000 which is obviously too slight (WS).

I have deliberately refrained from accepting the language of his verse as proof that Empedocles was not a Dorian. This language is a rich and colorful Ionian, studded here and there with words either local in usage or coined by himself. His language, however, is not a water-tight proof, because by his time certain Greek dialects had become standard for certain literary productions. Empedocles writes in dactylic hexameters—the meter of the epic poems (as, incidentally, does Parmenides)—so it was natural that he should have used the Ionic language. A certain doubt may linger in our minds, whether it was possible for a Dorian to have achieved such a perfection and intensity of expression in what was not his mother tongue. Hence we may consider Empedocles' beautiful Ionian as indicating a possibility (but not a proof) that he was not himself a pure Dorian.

Empedocles' Family. The name of Empedocles' father was probably Meton, a wealthy and influential citizen of Akragas. His grandfather, also called Empedocles, is reported to have won a victory at Olympia. This victory occurred in either a chariot race or a horse race of the Olympiad during which Empedocles the philosopher was born (FGH, IIB 241, fr. 7). The former is more likely, for foreignborn charioteers, sometimes even of foreign descent, took part in such races. Empedocles' father's name of Meton has been contested; first by Favorinus in his *Memorabilia*, who gives it as Archinomos, saying he had this information from a letter of Telauges, Pythagoras' son, to Philolaos (FHG, III, fr. 3). But Neanthes contests the authenticity of this letter (FGH,

IIA 84). As the name Archinomos occurs in no other source, we may dismiss this story. There is however another tradition credited to Satyros (FHG, III fr. 11), that Empedocles' father was called Exainetos, which Heraklides, son of Stration (VH, fr. 73, 76), tries to reconcile by saying that the son of Exainetos was another Empedocles, author of forty-six tragedies of which he himself knew forthy-three—whether by reading or by seeing them performed is not clear. But Neanthes insists on the identity of the philosopher and the tragedian, saying that he had personal knowledge of seven tragedies, and that Empedocles had composed them in his youth (FGH, IIA 84). Neanthes obviously intends to draw a parallel with the life of Plato.

Empedocles' Life and Personality. Raised in an affluent family and in prosperous surroundings, Empedocles appears to have shown from youth an insatiable curiosity and a will to emulate his most famous contemporaries and predecessors in the investigation of nature and in the shaping of a consistent picture of the world, which his rich imagination would later clothe in brilliant images and strikingly original expressions. It seems that he became a disciple of the Eleatic school quite early and that he afterwards turned to the study of the more remote doctrines of Heraclitus, of the early Milesians, and perhaps also of some oriental philosophies. Yet we have no reports of extensive early travels. He made several trips to southern Italy, but apparently did not venture so far afield as Egypt or Babylonia.

At a comparatively early age, Empedocles took an active part in politics and, after the death of his father, his democratic bent became more prominent. He was instrumental in overthrowing the oligarchy of "the Thousand" and in establishing a free democracy in Akragas. Unfortunately, the chroniclers and commentators, who indulge in useless details of banquets, descriptions of attire, and other tittle-tattle of this sort, omit—as if by a secret agreement among them all—to mention the date of such an important political event; although the recording system (related to the recurring Olympiads) was well established at this period and the fifth century was highly historically minded. Empedocles was almost the exact contemporary of Pericles; he was barely twenty years older than Socrates, a little older than Protagoras, and a little younger than Herodotus.

We do not know at what age Empedocles started to compose his first work *On Nature*, which bore the traditional title of other such works and was written in verse, like the works of his early teacher Parmenides. In contrast to other philosophers, he did not establish a school but concentrated his whole teaching upon one person, his friend Pausanias, a physician from Gela. Most of his predecessors had founded at least the rudiments of a school. Pythagoras had selected many men and women to be trained not only in those special sciences for which they showed a bent, but also in an austere and strictly regulated way of living in common.

Haughty and generous, Empedocles is reported to have carried out several public works at his own expense. This must surely have been after the overthrow of "the Thousand," during a period when his word had become law among his fellow citizens. Two of the most striking of such deeds can be recounted. When Akragas was plagued by a pestilence, Empedocles diagnosed the cause of it as the polluted wind coming down from a mountain gully. We are told he then ordered a number of asses to be killed and skinned, and their skins to be stretched over the narrowest part of the gully (FGH, IIA, 8h). Soon after this action, the sickness abated. This earned him the nickname of "wind stopper." As another instance, Empedocles diagnosed the cause of a pestilence affecting the neighboring city of Selinus as due to the polluted waters of the river traversing that city (DL, VIII, 70; VH, fr. 77). He had the course of two other rivers diverted so that they joined with the first, and by the swiftness of their combined currents the source of the pollution was swept away. This action shows a degree of wealth rare for a single citizen, and the act appears to have been selfless—a gratuitous gesture by a "grand seigneur"—for no mention can be found that Selinus rewarded him in any way. It did not even grant him citizenship when he was exiled by Akragas.

Both these actions must have taken place during the period

when "the Thousand" had been dismissed and Empedocles was head of the ruling democratic party. It is indeed reported by Aristotle himself, among other sources, that he was offered the crown of king, but that he refused it (ASE, fr. 66). This, Aristotle says, was the gesture of a truly free man, who preferred to live modestly rather than have the honors and luxury of a king. However, the two parts of Aristotle's praiseful comment do not necessarily cohere, as Empedocles lived anything but a modest life. Many near-miraculous cures were attributed to him, and Heraklides—whose credulity has already been mentioned—is reported by Satyros to have said that he, Heraklides, was present on one occasion when Empedocles was practicing magic (FGH, III fr. 12). The most astounding of his actions, which, as shown by the two public works already mentioned, seem to have been based on sound knowledge and practical ability, was the "resurrection" of a young woman. She had been given up for dead by all, and had remained for thirty days without breath or pulsebeat. Empedocles is said to have remained by her side day and night throughout this time, and in the end she recovered consciousness and revived. It may have been a case of catalepsy or severe concussion, and it is not impossible that, without his continuous presence, encouragement, and perhaps secret feeding, she might have passed from that state to death.

I have myself known of two cases in which the constant care and encouraging presence of a close relative performed such a near-miracle. The first was a boy who had fallen from a third-floor window and who was unconscious and given up by the doctors. His mother stayed near him for many days, refusing to abandon hope, constantly talking to him and attending to his bodily needs; and the boy revived. The second case was a woman who had a stroke and who was also doomed by medical opinion. Her daughter went on talking to her, feeding her, and behaving as if her mother was fully alive and could understand her; this woman also revived, though in a very weakened condition, and was able to eat and talk and read. I never saw her, but I knew the boy; he was a lively, normal youngster one year after his accident. These cases show that the functions of consciousness and of ability to respond to stimuli are quite distinct. Both could be considered miracles by naive observers.

Satyros reported that when the news went abroad that the young woman, Pantheia, had risen from her bed and was walking again, a group of people gathered at a banquet saw Empedocles approach and all rose and prostrated themselves before him as before a god. Banquets play a big part in the apocryphal traditions about Empedocles, and we shall refer again to them when we consider the legends built around him. Incidentally this girl, Pantheia, is one of the main characters in the tragedy by the German poet Hölderlin, *The Death of Empedocles*.

The only absolutely certain date we know of Empedocles' life is his journey to Thurii in 444 B.C., for its founding celebrations. Thurii, in Southern Italy, was a magnificent conception of Pericles. It was intended as an all-Greek colony with no "mother-city" to which it owed allegiance: a city to which any Greek could emigrate or in which he could take refuge, irrespective of his native city or his origin. Its founding celebrations in 444 B.C. were attended also by Herodotus, the great historian, and by Protagoras, the Sophist to whom Pericles had entrusted the drafting of the constitution of the city. The date is supposed to coincide with the time of Empedocles' "floruit," or prime of life, which was usually taken as the fortieth year. But if his birth occurred between 496–493 B.C. he was nearly fifty when he went to Thurii. He must in any case have been already well-known throughout the Greek world—and a prominent citizen of Akragas —to have been officially bidden to that occasion. Almost certainly he must at least have completed his first great work, *On Nature*, and probably he still ruled over Akragas, as he apparently returned there from Thurii.

The other certain event of his life, though not its date, is his visit to Olympia to hear his second great work publicly recited by a rhapsode named Cleomenes. But although these quadrennial games served as chronological sign-posts for Greek history, none of the sources tells us at which Olympiad this happened. Timaeus informs us that Empedocles' appearance caused more comment and more turning of heads than anyone else's (DL, VIII, 66; FHG, I, of the *Purifications* must have taken some time. We may therefore put at least eight years (two Olympiads) between Empedocles' (Some persons conscious of their superiority affect an uncommon mode of appearance, as an alternative to a self-consciousness that turns bitter because their merits may be insufficiently recognized.) a conversion does not take root in a moment, and the composition bronze sandals and a majestic tunic (DK, 31B fr. 112). In his attire and demeanor Empedocles has often been compared with Anaximander, the second of the three great Milesian philosophers. these notions are totally absent from his work *On Nature*. Such fr. 88a). As Empedocles describes himself in one of his fragments, he was crowned with the sacred fillets of the priests of Apollo, his arms laden with evergreen wreaths, and he wore his famous

The philosophical content of the *Purifications* that were recited at Olympia is in marked contrast to that of Empedocles' first work *On Nature*. We cannot but surmise that it was written after Empedocles' conversion to the Pythagorean doctrine of transmigration, hence to the idea of the immortality of the individual soul and to certain taboos that accompanied it, such as absention from meat and beans, a strict keeping of oaths, and a belief in sin. All journey to Thurii and his arrival at Olympia.* This tallies in part, but in part only, with Aristotle's report that Empedocles died as an exile in the Peloponnese around his sixtieth year. His triumphant progress through the crowds at Olympia does not in any way resemble the behavior of an exile; and, if he had died in the Peloponnese, Aristotle would have known more details about the place and time of his death. Piecing together the various contradictory reports, I am led to the following conclusions: Empedocles went to Olympia around the age of sixty, not fifty, and he was exiled "in absentia" by the descendants of the oligarchs he had overthrown a short generation before. After that, nothing positive is known of his movements, and this led Aristotle to the hypothesis that Empedocles died in the Peloponnese. From that point on, history gets thinner and the legends pullulate. Empedocles'

*W. Kranz still upheld the priority of the *Purifications* in his *Empedocles* (Zurich, 14949).

fragment whose beginning has been already quoted may have been written as the opening of *Purifications* (as it is placed by Diels-Kranz). On the other hand, it may well have been written to his friends at Akragas after the impression he had created at Olympia—an impression he was not loath to see repeated in many other "far-shining cities" in Sicily and Southern Italy after his return. We must remember that in those times exile was not a shameful fate; and that it was confined merely to the narrow limits of a single city state (usually an area less than a hundred miles across). In addition, it was easy for a man to have most of his fortune and belongings brought out to him in exile.

The scanty facts known of Empedocles' life have been adduced above. Even the sequence of events I have sketched out is not explicitly recorded by any commentator; it has had to be pieced together from bits of information scattered here and there. The time that elapsed between the overthrow of "the Thousand" and Empedocles' exile is usually reported as much shorter than I have indicated; but a remark of Diogenes Laertius has not been given its proper weight by the commentators. "Later," says Diogenes Laertius, "his return was opposed by his enemies' descendants"; which means that for at least a short generation—twenty years or so—Empedocles held sway over Akragas (DL, VII, 67).

To complete the scanty bits of information we have about Empedocles' life, we must draw upon the *banquets*. There are four stories of banquets, telescoped by many commentators into two. We have already mentioned one in which the guests rose and prostrated themselves before him as before a god. Empedocles cannot have been the host at that one. Then there is a garbled account of a banquet at which it is reported that Empedocles chided the master of ceremonies and later had him brought to trial and sentenced to death (FHG, I, fr. 88a). This could have been a way to get rid of a political opponent, though, even so, the notion seems unlikely; for no other story involving violent revenge is connected with Empedocles. The third concerns a feast Empedocles gave after his conversion to the Pythagorean conception of the transmigration of souls, hence to the belief that the sacrificial animal might have been a man in some previous existence, even a relative of his slaughterer. At this feast, the guests expected the usual sacrifice of a bull, which would be roasted and consumed by them after a leg had been burned to cinders as an offering to the gods. Instead they saw the effigy of a bull, made of flour, honey, and condiments (FHG, III, fr. 3).

Finally, there is the banquet after which Empedocles disappeared. This story is told in great detail by Heraklides, who however confuses it with the preceding banquet (VH, fr. 76). After a feast in the open air, he says, the guests lay down to sleep under the trees. (This feast is supposed to have been held in a field belonging to a certain Peisianax, a Syracusan, a story that has given rise to considerable, rather futile controversy.) Empedocles, however, is reported to have remained sitting or reclining in his place. But next morning he was nowhere to be found. When the servants were questioned, one said that during the night he had heard a voice calling Empedocles by name and that a brilliant light appeared on the summit of Aetna. This statement indirectly confirms that Empedocles must have been in exile at the time, for Akragas is not near enough to Aetna for it to be visible from there. It is also evidence that Empedocles could easily consort with his friends from Akragas and other places in Sicily, and that he still lived in comparative luxury. A search was then made and, near the top of the mountain, someone found one of his famous bronze, or bronze-studded, sandals. At this point Pausanias, his sole disciple, ordered the search to be called off, saying that what had happened was a fulfilment of prayer; Empedocles had now become a god, and they should all worship him as such. If all occurred as related, it is strange that Pausanias, who was quite wealthy, did not erect a cenotaph or an altar to Empedocles, as the inhabitants of Lampsacus had done for Anaxagoras.

Statements of Empedocles' age at the time of his death vary from sixty, the age given by Aristotle, to the improbable age of one hundred and nine. There is also a tale, quoted by Diogenes Laertius, that he died at the age of 77, having fallen from a chariot near Messina and broken his thigh (DL, VIII).

Diogenes Laertius includes two epigrams at the end of his life of Empedocles. Both are extremely prosaic and inartistic, but they show that, centuries after his time, Empedocles remained a live memory and a source of considerable curiosity. The first epigram, composed by Diogenes Laertius himself, tries to give a rational explanation of his fall into the crater of Mount Aetna:

> You too, once Empedocles, by the dire flame
> the body purifying, sought death in the crater's fire.
> I won't say you threw yourself deliberately into Aetna
> but that, wishing to escape attention, you fell into it advertently.

The second epigram by an unknown author gives the story of the chariot and the broken thigh:

> Tis true they say Empedocles fell from a chariot
> and broke his right thigh. If, on the other hand,
> he jumped into the crater and thus ended his life,
> how could then his grave be shown in Megara?

The "Megara" mentioned here is an Italiot city, a colony of the Megara in Attica. This epigram is odd, for many writers have commented on the absence of any grave, adding however that many other famous men have no known grave.

If in fact Empedocles did throw himself into the center of Mount Aetna, why did he? It cannot have been out of despair at his banishment from Akragas, for exile was a fairly common fate for prominent men in ancient Greece. The explanation may lie in his conviction that he possessed supernatural powers, and that men such as he could not die a natural death, but must be snatched up by the gods and translated into their rightful realm. In the *Purifications*, he states that such men:

> In the end become seers and composers of hymns,
> physicians and leaders of men on earth; from these states
> they sprout up again as gods immortal, honored above all.
>
> (DK, 31B fr. 146)

We shall notice, on studying his work more closely, that Empedocles claimed all these qualities for himself. That he was an accomplished physician and had probably conducted several autopsies is attested by the controversy in which he was engaged with followers of the Hippocratic school, who took him seriously enough to attempt to refute his statements. His *Purifications* might be considered as a series of hymns. We have also seen that Empedocles was prominent in politics, with a popular support strong enough to offer him the crown of king. In the first fragment of the *Purifications*, he mentions that, when he went through "the far-shining cities," he was followed by many who were in need of a prophecy or of a piece of comforting advice, being beset by many ills (DK, 31B fr. 112). In his opinion, such men should not be doomed to a common death and to decay as miserable corpses.

There were many stories in Greek mythology of men and women being bodily lifted up into "heaven" or to other realms. Iphigenia was saved by Artemis from immolation and wafted to Colchis to act as her priestess. Ganymede, the beloved of Zeus, was taken up to Olympus in the flower of his youth to serve the gods at their banquets. In quite another vein, Oedipus, that unhappy man who had unwittingly committed two most heinous crimes and suffered the utmost degradation, received an oracle that the land would be happy in which he met his death. He therefore travelled to Attica to reward Theseus for his hospitality, and was there annihilated by a thunderbolt. None of these left a corpse behind. The Greeks had a horror of the decay of a dead body, and funerals took place at night so that the sun should not look upon the dead man. We can be fairly sure that Empedocles longed for a similar death; but living in a more rationalist age, he was not sure it would be granted to him. So he forestalled fate by creating his own legend.

There may have been other causes for his action: satiety with life, the consciousness that he had given all of which he was capable, a feeling that his mental powers were on the wane, or simply a conviction that the time had come to go and meet his end. Suicide was not then considered a sin. It was accepted that, after mature deliberation, a man might end his life rather than live in a condition of reduced powers.

That Empedocles was far from being in such a state is attested by two fragments: the last fragment of *On Nature*, and the first of the *Purifications*. In the former he promises his sole disciple,

Pausanias, the acquisition of all the powers he had himself possessed; the second records his progress and the honor in which he was held.

> And all the medicines that are, to keep away old age and sickness
> thou wilt learn, for only to thee shall I these things reveal.
> Thou wilt stop the violence of tireless winds, which, rising
> out of the earth, destroy by their breath meadows and fields;
> and again, at thy will, new-risen winds will rush.
> From darkling rain wilt thou cause dry weather, appropriate to
>   men's needs,
> and in the drought of summer wilt thou call forth
> tree-nourishing streams and the branches will reach up to heaven.
> From the Netherworld thou wilt bring back the vital force of a
>   man already dead.
>
> (DK, 31B fr. 111)

The *Purifications* begins with the three lines (already quoted) addressing the citizens of Akragas, and then goes on:

> Hail! I wander among you now no more a mortal but like of god
>   immortal,
> honored by all, as is fitting, crowned with sacred fillets, laden
>   with wreaths.
> I am revered by men and women; thousands follow me as I go
>   through the shining cities.
> Some ask which is the way to gain; others are in dire need of a
>   prophecy;
> while others most desire to hear a word of advice
> To relieve their long-standing sufferings.
>
> (DK, 31B fr. 112)

Both these fragments show Empedocles at the height of his powers and full of self-confidence in his knowledge and art. They might indeed have been written in sequence and belong together. We shall see, in the rest of *Purifications*, that a definite and profound change has occurred in Empedocles' outlook which entitles us to suppose not only a lapse of some time between *On Nature* and the *Purifications*, but a sort of conversion to a new outlook, which can only have been occasioned by the influence of Pythagorean mys-

ticism. Empedocles' writing is as brilliant in *Purifications* as in his
first work, *On Nature*. Although one may deplore a certain nar-
rowing of Empedocles' detachment from personal fate and a return to certain older traditions that earlier he had seemed to have
overcome, his triumph at Olympia shows that he was still vigorous
in body and mind. (We reserve a comparison of the two works
for subsequent chapters.)

Despite the paucity and the contradictions of the extant information, the colorful and striking personality of the philosopher
has inspired many modern authors to attempt an imaginary reconstruction of his life, and to probe into the motives of his death.
The poet Hölderlin's tragedy in two acts, *The Death of Empedocles*, though weak in dramatic episode, manages to convey both
the greatness of the man and the frame of mind that could lead
him to seek a death for which he feels he is ready. Mathew Arnold's poem, "Empedocles on Aetna," also takes the legend of his
death for granted. Nietzsche refers to Empedocles repeatedly with
great admiration. Romain Rolland, in his monograph "Empedocle,
ou l'age de la haine," though understanding little of Empedocles'
philosophy, accepts that we are now in the period which Empedocles described as the mounting supremacy of Strife.

It is clear, even from the scanty information we possess, that
Empedocles was "a man of many parts," a universal mind of his
time: a distinguished physician, a prophet, a biologist, a man
prominent in politics, a benefactor of his own and neighboring
cities, a "grand seigneur" in his generosity, a great and original
poet, a convinced democrat, overbearing yet humble—as when he
described himself as a sinner, "a fugitive from the gods and a
vagrant." (DK, 31B, fr. 115)

Empedocles left no school. Pausanias, to whom he promised to
transmit all his powers, but about whom he had no illusions—
"thou shalt learn, yet no more than human mind can reach"—does
not seem to have been more than a good physician. (DK, 31B,
fr. 2) The only tenuous link of Empedocles with Athens is a
report that Pausanias came there during the Great Plague which
decimated the city's population at the beginning of the Peloponnesian war (429–428 B.C.), and that he was helpful in caring for

the stricken. An epigram to Pausanias is erroneously attributed to Empedocles. It runs:

> The physician called Pausanias, son of Anchites,
> an Asclepiad, native of Gela; many men, withering under baneful
> diseases were by his hand turned away
> from Persephone's realm in the Netherworld.

Though Empedocles visited Olympia, there is no record that he ever went to Athens. If he did, he might have made the same remark as Democritus, the great atomist who came from Abdera in Thrace, almost at the other end of the Greek world, and who, after visiting Athens, reported: "I went to Athens, but no one knew me"—meaning that no one took notice of him. For at that time, Athens had not yet become the center of philosophy, and was more or less the happy hunting ground of the Sophists. Before Plato, who raised the homely teaching of Socrates to immeasurable heights of metaphysical speculation, there was not a single major or minor philosopher who claimed Athenian citizenship.

In belated recognition of Empedocles' importance, his fellow citizens erected a statue to him in Akragas. Whether this happened before the destruction of the city by the Carthaginians in 404 B.C. or much later, when the city was repopulated under the Romans, we do not know. In any event, the statue is reported to have been removed from Akragas and reerected before the Senate House in Rome.

3. CONTEMPORARIES

The second half of the sixth and the first half of the fifth centuries B.C. saw the greatest expansion of the Greek race in the Mediterranean lands. Greek colonies studded the whole coast of Asia Minor and Sicily, and the southern part of Italy was so thickly strewn with them that the whole area was called Greater Greece. True, at the turn of the fifth century, Ionia was constantly assailed by Persian attacks; but, after the repulse of the Persians by Athens, Ionia was restored to peace, freedom, and wealth, and remained so for another 50 to 60 years. Indeed, one of the Ionian islands, Samos, was so strong that, in 440 B.C. under the leadership of Melissos, the last off-shoot of the Eleatics, it was able to endanger the Athenian Empire. The end of the Peloponnesian war (404 B.C.) saw an end to this prosperity. In the west, Greater Greece became a battleground between Rome and the Carthaginians, and one by one its cities fell, some to one, some to the other, but finally all to Rome. Syracuse held out for a century or so, under two tyrants, the elder and younger Dionysius, whom Plato tried vainly to encourage to build a new life on the solid basis of philosophic morality. In the east, the Spartans, the alleged defenders of Greek freedom, handed Ionia to the Persians. The populations, however, remained, and some cities even experienced a rebirth of their ancient well-being before Alexander reincorporated them all into the Greek world.

The period that concerns us here (the sixth and fifth centuries), was one of tremendous intellectual vigor. Many original ideas were propounded in Ionia and Greater Greece, and there was great freedom of interchange and a clash of crosscurrents within and between them. Contacts and exchanges also occurred with the non-Greek world—with the ancient wisdom of Egypt and Assyria and perhaps also India. Many philosophers were credited with long stays in Egypt (among them Pythagoras and Plato); Democritus is said to have made a journey to India and Scythia; and the historians Herodotus and Hecateus, to many other lands.

Thales the Milesian, the first Greek philosopher, is credited with a Phoenician mother—a descendant of Kadmos, the Phoenician king of Thebes. According to Plato's *Protagoras* (343), Thales arrived in Miletos after being exiled from Phoenicia with a certain Neilos. He had had no other teacher except the Egyptians, from whom he learned geography and geometry, like his successor Anaximander. The Milesian historian Hecateus (FGH, I,T, 12a, I,3) confirmed during his travels the exactness of Anaximander's map of the world. According to Herodotus, Pythagoras brought to Greek lands the doctrine of the Egyptians that the soul was immortal and migrated through all forms of animals during three thousand years. Plato in *Timaeus* has a long tale by Critias, of how his ancestor Solon visited and discoursed at length with the Egyptian priests. Plato's disappearance from Athens (and subsequently from Megara) after the execution of Socrates is of unknown duration, some estimating it as a few months; others, as three years. During this time he probably visited Egypt before going to Cyrenaica and then to the Pythagoreans in Italy; and the tale of Critias may well have been an account of Plato's conversations with the priests there.

This freedom of intercourse contrasts sharply with the later distinction between Greeks and barbarians. The population of the colonies had probably a great admixture of other races, as the people sent out from the respective metropolises were mostly unmarried men and language does not seem to have constituted the barrier it is sometimes made out to be: Themistocles, after taking refuge in Persia, learned the language perfectly in a single year. At the same time the purity, pliancy, and expressive power of the Greek language developed by leaps and bounds, until it became the most perfect instrument for expressing abstract thought.

The colonies flourished in lands where soil was richer than in Greece proper; hence they provided the margin necessary to the development of the apparently useless luxury of science and speculation. Of the cities on the Greek mainland, only Athens and Corinth could afford this luxury in the fifth century—but at what cost to themselves and to others!

This explains the enormous fees the Sophists asked for their tuition; they were accustomed to that sort of money. The Sophists Protagoras of Abdera, Gorgias from Leontini in Sicily, and Prodicos from the island of Kea were all "strangers to Athens." One is also left aghast at the enormous sum paid by the insignificant city of Abdera to Democritus, after he read to the citizens his great work, *The Great World Order*, on his return from his travels, having spent all his money.

All these cities were free of bondage to any Great Power, a fact that leads one to reflect on the relation of political freedom and creative thought. I venture to suggest that political freedom is a necessary prerequisite, though not sufficient in itself—and perhaps only when it is not made an excuse for wars, self-isolation, xenophobia, and the enslavement of others. The combination of implicit freedom, wealth, and intellectual ferment that existed during the period under consideration in both Ionia and Greater Greece can be compared to the richness and variety of Italian culture during the early Renaissance. Athens knew magnificently how to exploit the freedom she enjoyed for about sixty years after she had reduced the Persian threat. Such privileged periods seem to occur rarely and intermittently in human history. They cannot be created at will; apparently, the more a state strives consciously for "culture," the more that elusive quality escapes it.

The overall picture of Empedocles' times, from the philosophical point of view, may be sketched as follows: By the time of his birth, most of the principal schools of philosophy had already been established, and still continued to flourish. The three great Milesian philosophers—Thales, Anaximander, and Anaximines—were already dead; but, although nothing of the work of Thales was preserved, probably parts of the works of the others were accessible. For example, a remote connection cannot be ruled out between Empedocles and the theories of the Milesians; such a connection is indicated by some of Empedocles' preoccupations, especially his physiology. It is also true that Empedocles (as already mentioned) is reported to have imitated the majestic garb and haughty demeanor of the second Milesian, Anaximander; but this, if true at all, must have been on the basis of hearsay, since Apollodorus reports Anaximander's death to have occurred shortly after 546 B.C., before Empedocles was born, and Empedocles is not known to have visited Asia Minor. (FGH, IIB, 244)

The Eleatic School. It is most probable that Empedocles had a direct and early contact with the Eleatic school in Southern Italy. If we leave out of consideration the strange personality of Xenophanes, who was among the founders of the colony of Elea, the real founder of the Eleatic school was Parmenides. According to the Platonic dialogue that bears his name, Parmenides was already sixty-five when he came to Athens in 450 B.C. with his disciple Zeno, who was then about forty years of age. Parmenides there expounded his doctrine in a discussion with the young Socrates, then twenty years old, whom he showed how to handle a subject of dialectics. His companion, Zeno, was a famous expounder of paradoxes. He is said to have composed forty of these, four of which have been preserved, regarding the impossibility of conceiving movement. These four still exercise the ingenuity of mathematicians and logicians. If the story of the dialogue between Parmenides and Socrates is based on historic fact, Zeno must have been a few years younger than Empedocles. Zeno, according to Suidas (DL, IX,29), wrote an "Explanation" of Empedocles' doctrine for the 82nd Olympia (448–445 B.C.); and, according to Aristotle (ASE, fr. 65), Zeno discovered or invented dialectics, and Empedocles rhetoric.

I must emphatically disagree with the second part of this statement. Rhetoric is compared by Plato to the art of the confectioner, that flatters the palate without regard to the health of the consumer. It is the art of covering ignorance with seemingly rational arguments; in a word, it is an art of deceit. An orator can present an argument or its contradiction in such a way that he convinces the listener he is telling the truth. Hence, at bottom, the orator believes in nothing and has no theory of his own to expound. It is true that there are several original and striking expressions in Empedocles' work—turns of phrase invented by him—but he was not a rhetorician. He was a dedicated philosopher who tried to arrive at truth, turning his subject now this way and now that, even occasionally lighting verbal fireworks. Aristotle, who, as much as Plato, combated the whole band of Sophists, long since dead, no doubt intended his comment on Empedocles as derogatory; but Aristotle also made a statement that, historically speaking, may absolve him.

Aristotle states that Gorgias, leading citizen of Leontini, and one of the greatest Sophists of the fifth century, was at one time Empedocles' disciple. This Gorgias was sent to Athens by his fellow citizens in 427 B.C. to ask for Athenian aid for his city against the Syracusans. He later established a school in Thessaly, living there to an advanced old age, and is supposed by many classical scholars to have influenced Thucydides. Now, there is no author in Greek literature less rhetorical than Thucydides, whose every sentence is wrung out of him after long deliberation, in a difficult, dense, and original language. So at the two ends of the line Empedocles-Gorgias-Thucydides, we have highly eminent men and original thinkers, and in between them a so-called orator. This does not make sense, unless Gorgias was more than a mere Sophist. Indeed, many of the Sophists were philosophers, sociologists, psychologists, and linguists. One would like to think that an intellectual influence was passed on by the non-Dorian Gorgias, transmitting to Thucydides something of the thought of Empedocles.

To return to Parmenides: The Eleatic school represents the most consequential and uncompromising monism in the whole history of philosophy. Reality, or Being, is one indivisible whole—eternal, immutable, and immobile. There is no void; to speak of void is to speak about nothing; about nothing, nothing can be said. Being has no parts, hence it cannot even move within itself.

Parmenides has an expression, unusual in philosophic works: "Don't sit there gaping. . . . (mortals) are driven anyhow, both blind and deaf; gaping tribes without judgment." (DK 28B fr. 6) And an Empedoclean fragment states:

> Do thou look (at these things) with thy mind, and don't sit there gaping in amazement at what thine eyes show thee.
>
> (DK 31B fr. 17)

The use of the same words cannot be accidental. But though a contempt for the direct evidence of the senses and for the power of understanding of the common man is shared by many philosophers, its repercussions on the theory of knowledge of these two philosophers, Parmenides and Empedocles, are very different.

While Parmenides denied all evidence of the senses, Empedocles admitted them as means of carrying, not immediate conviction, but the first rudiments on which philosophic speculation must build, after a long process of sifting. But the repetition of the same word shows that the influence of the Eleatics remained in the background, having entered the receptive mind of a young man.

Another point of apparent resemblance between Parmenides and Empedocles is the theory of the Sphairos. For Parmenides, the immovable universe is in the shape of a sphere:

> But as there is an outermost limit set fast on all sides,
> it is complete, comparable in mass to a well-rounded sphere,
> all round, at an equal distance from the centre; it cannot grow
> a little greater or a little less, this way or that.   (DK 28B fr. 8)

And Empedocles:

> In it were not to be seen the swift limbs of the sun
> nor the earth's dense vegetation; nor yet the sea.
> So much was the Sphairos firmly embedded
> within the secret compactness of harmony, spherical all round,
> exultant in surrounding solitude.   (DK 31B fr. 27)*

*I borrow the last sentence, "exultant in surrounding solitude," from W.E. Leonard's translation of the fragments of Empedocles, which, though often inaccurate and lacking in philosophical understanding, at times includes happy renderings.

But he, on all sides equal and altogether infinite,
the rounded Sphairos, exultant in surrounding solitude.

(DK 31B fr. 28)

The next fragment stresses the utter dissimilarity of the Sphairos
to a man's (or a god's) body:

From its back no twin branching arms are swinging;
it has no feet or swift-moving knees, or sexual organ shaggy,
It is a sphere, on all sides equal unto itself.   (DK 31B, fr. 29)

The differences are already apparent. In one of Empedocles'
fragments the Sphairos is unlimited on all sides, yet equal to itself;
modern mathematics admits of equal and unequal infinite numbers.

The dissimilarity of the Sphairos to the human shape may be a
remoter echo from Xenophanes, alleged by some to be the first
Eleatic philosopher. This is doubtful, for there are no traces in the
austere doctrine of Parmenides of Xenophanes' jovial, disrespect-
ful treatment of all the time-hallowed traditions of the Greeks,
the gods, the honored athletes, etc.

Xenophanes lived beyond the age of 92, an itinerant rhapsode,
singing his own verses full of derision for the old poets, Homer
and Hesiod, and for all traditional forms of worship. "If bulls and
lions had hands," he says, "they would have made images of the
gods in their own likeness." (DK 21B, fr.15) He wrote not only
in dactylic hexameters, but also the shorter Silloi satyrical verses
against all and sundry. Xenophanes is also credited with the saying, considered so original in Socrates' Apology, that he had done
more good to men than the athletes, victorious at Olympia because
of their swiftness of foot or strong fists. What interests us in
connection with Empedocles is his conception of the Sphairos,
which is fundamental to Empedocles' theory of the cosmic cycle.
For Xenophanes (according to Aristotle), the Sphairos is the form
of the divine: a sphere neither finite nor infinite; all-mind, all-
seeing, all-hearing, but not breathing, having nothing in common
with the human species. (AMP I, v, 986b) For Parmenides, as we
have seen, the Universe as a whole is a sphere, immobile, un-

changeable, the only Being which cannot have originated from anything else; nor can it change since it would then become something other than itself; that is, Not-being. For Xenophanes, the Sphairos exists outside the world, and is therefore transcendent and simultaneous with the universe. For Empedocles this becomes one of four phases of the cosmic cycle, which is periodically destroyed and reformed. The Universe becomes the Sphairos when it gathers everything unto itself, and there are no gods, or beasts, or men, or earth, or sky, or sea.

Another trace of Xenophanes' teaching in Empedocles is his acceptance of the four elements, earth, air, fire, and water. However, this was a common tenet of many philosophers at that time, as well as of the Hippocratean school of medicine, and Aristotle is wrong in attributing the addition of the fourth element—earth— to Empedocles.

We may conclude, from all so far said, that the influence of the Eleatics was pretty strong at a certain stage of Empedocles' development. But it never went very deep, for the few fragments quoted to verify this influence are in contradiction with the rest of his theory. In Empedocles' work, logical force of argument, which constituted the paramount and original contribution of the Eleatic school, is more and more pushed aside in favor of a grandly imaginative and intuitive conception of the Universe and its laws. In this conception, change in quality as well as in quantity (perhaps not of the whole but of its parts), movement, and striving go on forever, creating all the time new forms. Although the immobile, changeless perfection of the Sphairos does occur, it does so only at immeasurably long intervals, and it lasts for a limited stretch of time. Empedocles cares less about logical consistency that about an internal metaphysical consistency. He maintained his reverence for Parmenides throughout his life, and never explicitly repudiated the influence of the Eleatics, but engulfed or amalgamated it into a more synoptic picture of the Universe.

Heraclitus. It is impossible to understand the development of Empedocles' thought without taking into account the influence of Heraclitus, from far-away Ephesus in Asia Minor. Historically,

Empedocles could not have come into direct contact with Heraclitus, for we have no reports of his journeying to Asia Minor. Heraclitus published nothing during his lifetime, and very early earned the nickname of "the obscure." From the scanty fragments that have been preserved, he did not bother to develop his arguments, but talked in short, pithy apothegms, embodying the meeting and merging of logical opposites. The apothegms were therefore seemingly paradoxical, inverting the logical process and deliberately asserting contradictory statements, which he believed to be a more accurate expression of reality.

Dialectics in the Hegelian sense, according to which a state of affairs and of thought inevitably produces its own contradiction, and then merges with it to produce a higher synthesis, thus becoming a new thesis to be later overturned by a new contradiction, and so on ad infinitum, must certainly be attributed to Heraclitus. He, however, did not consider *time* as the element of such a development, but thought of the contradictions existing simultaneously. His was the second main influence which Empedocles received, and it determined his theory much more deeply than the Eleatic doctrine.

In character and mood Heraclitus was almost the exact opposite of Empedocles. He despised the great mass of mankind: "one is to me worth ten thousand." He believed in no salvation or expiation of sin, except by a restoration at the final conflagration through Dike, Justice—the impersonal Logos. Although the law of the universe is "common"—that is, it is patently open for all people to see, if only they have enough sense to become aware of it—each individual thinks he has a mind of his own. But there will come a time, when Dike "will judge all"; when the world will go up in flames from which perhaps a new universe will emerge. Better? Worse? He does not bother with these moral qualifications. He offers nothing but his naked, deep, and wounded thought; for the sake of which (in this alone like Empedocles) he had resigned a kingship in favor of his brother. This was probably a ceremonial kingship connected with the worship of Artemis. In Heraclitus' contempt for mankind he at times included himself and this made him wish to humiliate his own person. However, he was not devoid of public spirit; for while Ephesus was besieged by the Persians, and the Ephesians, though threatened by shortage of food, continued to live luxuriously, he came to the public assembly with a bowl of flour mixed with water, and ate it without words in view of everyone. The lesson was taken to heart; food was rationed to the bare necessities, and the Persians raised the siege, realizing that it would have to last a long time.

The Eleatics preached the absolute immobility and immutability of the real world, but Heraclitus advanced, with zest and fanaticism, the reality of change. There is no real identity of things or of persons: "You cannot bathe twice in the same river, both it and yourself will be different, on the two occasions." (DK, 22B, fr.91) The apparent identities are in reality different, and the apparent differences are identical. He scoffed at the distinctions made by philosophers and by quasi-philosophers like Hesiod, "who did not even know that Night and Day are the same thing, yet arrogantly composed a cosmogony. On the other hand two moments of the same process are totally different." All "becoming" originates in the clash of opposites, and "war is the father of all things." (DK 22B, fr. 53) But over the war and the clash of opposites presides the universal Reason, Cause, and Thought— the Logos. This is "common" in the sense that it exists in and permeates all phenomena; not, as interpreted by some modern commentators, because it is a universal language, common, to all men, and a product of life in society. On the contrary, Heraclitus claims that he alone knew and and could explain "the nature of everything and telling how each thing is; while people are without wisdom, both before hearing the truth and after they have heard it. They do not understand what they do in waking life, as they are unconscious of what they (do) in sleep"; and "while the Logos is common, the mass of mortals live as if they had a mind of their own." (DK 22B, fr. 1,2) Also, "the harmony which results from opposites is better than any other" and "the harmony which is not perceptible by the senses is better than the obvious harmony." Not only are the apparent opposites one and the same thing—"the way up and the way down is the same"—but the radical changes from life to death, from sleep to waking, unite in the Logos while the apparent things "give an account and take revenge on each other according to the eternal Dike." (DK 22B, fr. 28,60)

These paradoxes are not inspirations of an enthusiastic moment. Heraclitus abhors and ridicules the manic cults: the smearing with blood to atone for bloodshed. Dionysos to him is not the god of resurrection, but is identical with Hades, the realm of Death. Heraclitus reached to the outermost limits of the mind, where ideas inebriate, where insight makes one mad.

The Heraclitean teaching wrenched and liberated Empedocles from the sterile repetition of the Eleatics, which offered no prospect of any deeper understanding with its negation of all movement, all change. He considered all such phenomena as appearances belonging to the world of "opinion," hence essentially to non-being, of which nothing can be said.

Empedocles did not adopt Heraclitus' teaching wholesale. He brought into it considerable innovations of his own, and probably thought that he could ultimately reconcile the two doctrines in a superior synthesis. His elements, "running through each other, take on various forms and shapes, so much does the mixture change them"; but so far as they periodically return to the same pattern, they are eternally and forever the same. (DK 31B, fr. 21) In the place of dead immobility, he proclaims the cosmic cycle, in which the earth, the sun, men, beasts and planets, even the gods, are transitory expressions.

These two influences, the Eleatic doctrine and the Heraclitean change, may be considered as the two major influences apparent in Empedocles' first work: *On Nature*. At a certain moment of his life after pondering on these things long and "with true intent" as he advises his disciple to do, Empedocles must have conceived his original picture of the universe, which united change with eternity, variety with immutability. This moment must have come to him in early maturity. For he must already have become well-known as a philosopher, before he was invited to Thurii and before Anaxagoras and Zeno—both a few years younger than himself—wrote treatises in explanation of his system.

The problem is often raised of how Heraclitus could have exerted such a deep-going influence upon Empedocles, while separated from him geographically, racially, and politically. There are no records of any direct contact between the two men, and the completed work of Heraclitus never saw the light of day. Heraclitus had taken the precaution of depositing his work in the temple of Artemis at Ephesus, from whence it was later stolen by a certain Crates, allegedly a student of the Platonic Academy; and after that it disappeared. But this difficulty of contact really presents no problem. We tend to minimize the extent of commercial, social, and cultural traffic between the two ends of the Greek world. Refugees from the numerous islands of the Aegean and from the shores of Asia Minor flocked continuously to the new cities of Greater Greece. Ideas were then not dead signs on paper, but live forces, percolating through the minds of men, and setting them to work. The doctrines of Heraclitus, although famous for their "obscurity," were easily remembered because of their sharp insight and their pithy expressions. Further, though no special study has yet been made of the subject, Heraclitus' work embodied diffuse ideas from the older philosophies of the East. The Persian Empire extended to Egypt on the South, and to the borders of India on the East.

The Pythagorean School. The Pythagorean school in Southern Italy, first established at Croton, exercised a strong attraction for many circles in Greater Greece. Its austerity of life and strict moral code, as well as its acceptance of male and female disciples from all Greek races—and even from the barbarians—went against the customs and prejudices of the time. Its period of greatness may be dated with some accuracy between 504 and 501 B.C.; but, apart from that, almost complete chaos reigns as to the chronology of Pythagoras himself and of his main disciples.

It seems that Pythagoras, a native of Samos, came to South Italy around 540 B.C., fleeing the rule of the tyrant Polycrates, who had taken control of the island. Whether he had visited Egypt and became acquainted with Egyptian and other eastern religions on the way, is not certain. However, it is clear that his doctrine was already fully developed in his mind, and that his school flourished for nearly forty years. The story that political opponents, led by

the oligarch Kylon, burned down the building within which most
of the adepts were gathered may possibly be true; but the story
that only two escaped because of their youth and nimbleness, is
highly improbable in view of the wide proliferation of the Pythagorean doctrine and the maintenance of its unity and coherence
for some eight to ten generations of scholars. "Generations" must
here be taken as scholarly generations, reflecting that new groups
of adepts joined the school every ten or fifteen years. The discipline
was that of a religious order, with a sort of excommunication put
into effect for any disciples who disclosed any of the secret or
esoteric tenets of the theory. After the date of the burning, Pythagoras himself disappears completely from the scene, though he
was not in the building at the time but had gone to Metapontium.
The legendary elements that have surrounded his name ever since
lie outside our subject.

Empedocles, if he was in fact connected with the Pythagorean
school, must have known men of the second or even the third
generation of Pythagoreans. Among those with whom his name
has been associated were Telauges (the son of Pythagoras) and
Philolaos. The Neoplatonist Porphyry, who lived nearly a thousand years after the events we are trying to reconstruct, states
that Empedocles in his youth was the beloved either of Parmenides
or of Telauges, the son of Pythagoras (NP, fr. VIII). Telauges,
even if assumed to be a child of Pythagoras' old age, must have
been considerably older than Empedocles. Telauges is further unlikely as an influence, from the inner evidence of the Empedoclean
fragments, which show that Empedocles came under the influence
of the Pythagorean doctrine only in his maturity. Philolaos is also
an enigmatic figure. According to Neanthes, Philolaos and Empedocles were the first to divulge the secrets of the Pythagorean
doctrine. (FGH, IIA 8) If so, Philolaos cannot have belonged
to that generation that heard Pythagoras himself teach. After
their disclosures, the report continues, it was forbidden to
communicate the innermost secrets to the outer circle of adher-
ents. Another incredible story purports that Philolaos went to
Thebes to perform the funeral rites for Lysis, who had been both
his teacher and the teacher of Epaminondas, the Theban general

of the first half of the 4th century B.C. A still more fantastic story tells how Plato, during his second stay in Syracuse at the court of the tyrant Dionysius the Younger in 367 B.C., bought from the aging and destitute Philolaos the three secret books of Pythagoras for a comparatively moderate sum. For technical reasons which it would take too long to relate here, it cannot have happened during his first journey in 388 B.C. It is absolutely impossible that Philolaos, who must have been more or less a contemporary of Empedocles, could have been alive at either of these dates, or that he should have heard Pythagoras himself lecture. More credible is the report that Plato bought the books from surviving relatives of Philolaos. This story, if true, makes Plato's responsibility still heavier for the loss of the Pythagorean written tradition. For he had a school, and could have set some of his disciples to copy the Pythagorean books as well as his own, which are so fully preserved.

The Pythagorean doctrine was a strange but vital amalgam of scientific mathematics, Eastern beliefs in the transmigration of the soul, a dose of asceticism and various taboos. At the end of each day, the disciples confessed whatever they had done that they ought not to have done, and whatever they had omitted to do that they ought to have done. The school produced many generations of scientists and technicians of all sorts: mathematicians, architects, physicians, townplanners, etc. I have ventured elsewhere to suggest that the perfection of the acoustics in the great theatres of the 5th and 4th centuries B.C. may have been due to the secret geometrical formulas of the Pythagoreans. Empedocles does not seem to have been interested at all in the mathematical side of the doctrine, which exercised a strong influence on Plato. But he adopted the metaphysical theory of the transmigration of souls, hence of the immortality of the individual soul, and also part of the taboos—forbearance from meat and bloody sacrifice, as well as from beans etc. He also adopted the deeper notion of sin, until then practically unknown to the Greek mentality. All this must have been absorbed during Empedocles' late maturity, after his fiftieth year; for there is no trace of such things in his first work, *On Nature*.

The Triangle. The Eleatic, Heraclitean, and Pythagorean schools of thought all contributed to Empedocles' development, and he seems to have extracted from each whatever suited his own conception. His "one universe" is very different from that of Parmenides, his "eternal return" very different from that of Heraclitus, and his conversion, late in life, to the Pythagorean transmigration of souls is again something quite different from the four lives which Pythagoras is said to have remembered.

These three original sources of knowledge, attitude of mind, and ideas may be pictured as a triangle, between whose sides Empedocles' thought weaved its pattern. Reversing the chronological order of the emergence of these doctrines, we must accept, on the internal evidence of his work, that the influence of the Eleatic Parmenides was the first, and the least potent. Empedocles next received the "effluvia," as he might have put it, from the Heraclitean teaching, which exercised a much more decisive influence that remained with him throughout his life, though diffuse and less easily detectible by quotation of chapter and verse. Last came the Pythagorean doctrines, in a kind of illumination, causing a conversion of thought and feeling, in which he tried very hard to salvage parts of his earlier but mature work: *On Nature.* A new turn was given to his mind. He saw the human soul in dire trouble and in need of direction. It was after this that he composed the *Purifications* and it was this new faith that enabled him to go and meet his own death calmly, almost triumphantly. His admiration for Pythagoras is expressed in a few lines, which might well serve as a fitting epitaph for that great man:

> There was one man among them, who knew more than any one
> and possessed the largest wealth of intellectual power.
> Able most of all to perform all kinds of wise actions.
> For when that man would tense his whole intellectual power,
> he could easily *see* each one of the totality of things,
> easier than ten men in twenty lives.   (DK 31B fr. 12)

The triangle of these three influences has a narrow base, linking Elea with Croton or with Metapontium or whatever other center the Pythagoreans established as their headquarters after the destruction of their original school. The two other much longer sides of the triangle converge at a very acute angle on the far-away city of Ephesus. Perhaps they never quite met, the triangle being open toward the east to admit of still remoter influences from the purer and more single-minded devotion of the Indians to abstract contemplation and an austere life.

Like his elements, which change their appearance when they enter into different mixtures, Empedocles took a great deal from his three great predecessors but produced a "mixture" peculiar to himself: a system original, coherent, and striking. This is exactly what the Greeks as a whole did with all the elements they borrowed from the wisdom of Egypt, Babylon, and other oriental sources. The so-called pre-Socratics in fact prepared a sort of blueprint of modern European philosophy. There is hardly a theory or a system that is not at least hinted at: monism, dualism and pluralism, extreme materialism and absolute idealism; man as the center of the world and man as an inconspicuous creature doomed to dissolution like all other forms of life; divinity as the all-powerful dominion over nature and as a creation of human inventiveness; one world, or many living unknown to each other; pantheism and monotheism, etc. etc. These are the categories within which philosophical speculation was to move through the ages. It is as if the early Greeks sketched out the boundaries within which the human mind can function and work. Modern thought still seems to strive in vain for a new train of ideas, a new direction in which to lead its aspirations.

4. PHYSICS AND METAPHYSICS

Empedocles, as we have seen, is considered a "pluralist" in that he does not assume *one* primeval stuff to be at the root of all things, as did the three great Milesians in the century before him. The first of these was Thales; he maintained that the basic stuff out of which all things originate was water or moisture. Aristotle's explanation is that Thales was led to this view because of the liquid nature of all animal semen, and because if things are deprived of all moisture they shrivel up and die. Thales had a wide range of interests. He took an active part in constructing the fortifications of his city, and in guiding its politics away from meddling in the quarrel between the Lydians and the Persians. This resulted in Miletus being spared after the Persian victory. He is credited with a Phoenician mother, descended from the royal house of Kadmos. To him are attributed many scientific discoveries: he is said to have discovered the Little Bear and the Tropics and the solstices, as well as to have fixed the year's length at 365 days. If this had been adopted, much confusion would have been avoided between the calendars of the various peoples (even of the various cities). His prediction of an eclipse in the reign of King Darius is precisely dated by modern astronomy. He also is said to have written a work on "nautical astrology," a guide to navigation by the stars. Born in 686 B.C. Thales was proclaimed one of the Seven Sages in 582. He was greatly admired by Herodotus, Xenophanes (who scoffed at nearly everyone else), Heraclitus, and Democritus. (FGH, IIB 228 fr. 1; HE, I 74/75; DK, 21B fr. 19, 22B fr. 58, 68B fr. 115a)

Thales' successor, Anaximander, who died about 545 B.C., took a great leap forward in considering that the basic stuff of all natural things was not a material element (water) but an abstract idea (the Infinite) out of which all things originate. Hence he posited infinitely many worlds, independent of each other, and a continuous becoming and decaying of every such world. He proclaimed that the earth was round, lying in the middle of the universe. He is reported to have made the first map of the then known terrestrial world, which was later to be confirmed by the historian and great traveler Hecataeus as well as by Herodotus. This may seem to us a simple matter, but to conceive that the three-dimensional mountains, oceans and cities of the world could be pictured on a plane surface represented a daring innovation. Anaximander's leap from a tangible and visible substance (water) to an abstract Infinite was shunned by most later Greek philosophers; Pythagoras identified the "indefinite dyad" with all that was to be avoided. We saw how Parmenides insisted that the world was immensely large, but finite, and how Empedocles repeated this assertion with a weaker voice. If the world is infinite, and its parts act on each other, it becomes impossible to establish strict laws governing the particular phenomena. Anaximander seems to have accepted this indefiniteness, for he maintained that the parts of the universe are in constant movement, yet the whole remains immobile. Simplicius, one of the more reliable commentators, when reporting the above, adds that Anaximander was the first to coin the word "infinite" (apeiron), whose nature was different from that of water or any other matter. (DOX, 476) From it were formed the sky and many universes, which decayed according to the law of time. Traces of this theory will be found in Empedocles' views, though in a different form.

The leap into the abstract was too great. Anaximander's successor, Anaximenes, although keeping the notion of the Infinite, reverted to the idea of a primeval "stuff" that had a remote connection with sense perception: air. He taught that it was air that, by condensation and rarefaction, creates the clouds, the rain (water), then the earth and stones and metals, all of which finally return to it by rarefaction.

The chief characteristic of the three Milesians was that they were all monists, and reduced all phenomena to transformations of one material underlying all things.

Heraclitus, whose home at Ephesus lay not very far from Miletus, though he had no apparent connection with the Milesian school, may also be called a monist. Fire was for him the beginning and the end of everything: "as all things are exchanged for gold, and gold for all things, so it is with fire." (DK, 22B fr. 90) Fire is, however, both a stuff and a process. Both Aristotle (AMP, I, iii, 98a) and Simplicius (DOX, 475) are explicit on this point. "Hipponicos of Metapontium (probably Pythagorean) also believed the origin of all things to be one, limited and in movement, and made fire the beginning of all things . . . and they made all things end in fire." In this respect Heraclitus is very near modern astronomy, which explains the formation of stars by explosions. Anaximenes was also credited with many discoveries, and it is at times difficult to discriminate which of them should be attributed to which Milesian.

Not a single genuine quotation has come down to us from any of the great Milesians. That they were searchers into natural phenomena is beyond doubt. In a sense, Empedocles continued their tradition.

The Elements. Aristotle, basing himself on the traditions of the Milesians and of Heraclitus, and disregarding the Infinite of Anaximander, maintains that it was Empedocles who added to the three already known elements—water, air, and fire—the most palpable of all, earth. (AMP I, 3, 984a). Simplicius concurs, relying on Theophrastus' *Physical Opinions* (DOX, 475). However, as already noted, Xenophanes, the near-centenarian from Kolophon, seems to have been the first to put forward a theory of the four elements; although, according to Diogenes Laertius, the theory actually stems from further back in time (DL, IX. 19, VIII. 10). He states that it was held by Manethos as well as by the historian Hecataeus, adding that they had both acquired it from Egypt, and that they believed the four elements were originally merged in one primeval stuff—"matter"—and were later separated from it.

Among many of the older pre-Socratic philosophers, there is controversy or rather doubt whether there were four or five elements: some differentiate between fire and ether, other between ether and air.

Though the distance in time between Empedocles and Aristotle was a little more than a century, the work of all the pre-Socratics seemed to Aristotle to belong to an entirely different era from his own. Aristotle's own world was bounded by the Sophists, the Platonic school, and the various off-shoots of the Socratic method, the Cynics, the Eristics of Megara, and others. Although he refutes all of them on certain points, they were all concerned with problems similar to his own, and he abhorred the idea of an infinite constitution of the universe with many universes coming into being and perishing unknown and unknowable to one another.

Empedocles swings from the Eleatic conception of a finite, though immensely large, universe, which also suffers periodic destruction and recreation, to the idea of the infinite, which renders all things indefinite. On the whole, except for one or two fragments testifying to the contrary, he comes down on the side of the finite quantity of the stuff of the Universe, since he repeatedly stresses that, from nothing, nothing can be born, and that nothing really perishes, though mortals consider the dissolution of things and creatures as "dire death."

The only immortal and indestructible things are in reality the four elements. Empedocles does not call them "elements," the "stoicheion" having in all probability been coined by Aristotle. Empedocles calls them "roots" (rizomata).

The coming into being and the dissolving into the primeval elements is continuous in Empedocles' view. It never ends, taking now one form, now another. The state of the world is in perpetual flux. But then again, it is perpetually the same, since the same conditions return periodically. The periods may be very long; but, in view of eternity, length of time is irrelevant. It is not clear whether Empedocles knew of Pherekydes' theory, who made time one of the three primeval and eternal forces that existed before the gods, or light, or the oceans. Pherekydes is considered by some scholiasts as Pythagoras' teacher, and they date his "floruit" as

540 B.C., while others push his birth back to 600 B.C. Empedocles considers that as the four elements, by mixing with each other, produce all things and all creatures, the latter are all transient and doomed to disappear. Thoughtless men call this disappearance death, and their coming together birth, and they lament or rejoice accordingly. On this occasion, as on many others, Empedocles lays stress on the mental short-sightedness of men, whose small existence is ephemeral, and who perish miserably, having understood nothing of the real essence of the world.

But let us first consider the fragment in which the word "rizomata" occurs:

> Of the roots of all things hear me first speak:
> Zeus the white splendour, Hera carrying life, and Aidoneus,
> and Nestis, whose tears bedew mortality.   (DK, 21B fr. 8)*

Much controversy has been caused by this fragment: Whether Zeus means fire, or the ether; whether Hera is the earth or the air; and what does Aidoneus really stand for? In my opinion, Zeus certainly represents the sun, the source of light and fire; Hera cannot but be the earth, which carries or supports all life. If so, only air remains for Aidoneus, who in mythology is the ruler of the Netherworld. Some traditions give this realm to Dionysus but, according to Heraclitus, they are one and same deity. Nestis was a local Sicilian deity of rivers and springs later worshipped as the goddess of sobriety. Her name means literally "fasting." Hippolytus (according to Plutarch) gives an ingenious interpretation: that Nestis is the water, which carries and dissolves food though it does not nourish, and that Aidoneus is the air, through which we see everything, though it has no light of its own.

This habit of Empedocles to designate his elements and, as we shall see, also his forces with names of gods and other mythological beings is unfortunate, for it leads to confusion. It was probably fragments such as this that caused Aristotle to remark that Empedocles is "Homeric" because he uses metaphor and all

---

*I borrow the expression "whose tears bedew mortality" from Leonard's translation of the fragments of Empedocles. It is one of his happy phrasings.

the other devices of the poetic art. (ADP, fr. 70) However, I consider such passages merely quasi-poetic, while other passages that speak of the elements, the forces, and the process using their proper terms and names are real poetry; for example, the following lines from the very important and longest fragment, whose beginning with its stress on apparently contradictory statements reminds us of Heraclitus:

> I shall speak a double truth; at times
> one alone comes into being;
> at other times, out of one several things grow.
> Double is the birth of mortal things and double their demise.
> For the coming together of all both causes their birth
> and destroys them; and separation nurtured in their being
> makes them fly apart. These things never stop changing
> throughout.   (DK, 31B fr. 17, l. 1-6)

and further down in the same fragment:

> They (elements) are for ever themselves, but running
> through each other they become at times different, yet are
>   for ever
> and ever the same.   (DK, 31B fr. 17, l. 34-35)

A sign of the confusion that set in very early in the interpretation of the pre-Socratics is the fact that Aristotle, after mentioning the four elements, adds that Empedocles reduced them to two, lumping earth, air, and water together and contrasting them with fire, from which they originate and to which they return. (AGC, 330b 20; AMP, I. iv. 985a 25) There is not a trace of such a view in the existing fragments, nor in the writings of any other commentators. The statement may be due to a confusion with Heraclitus, but how Aristotle could confuse the two is difficult to understand.

The verse "double is the birth of mortal things and double their demise" is of the essence of Empedocles' whole theory, and the root of most of its misinterpretations. I think it may be interpreted as follows: in the initial or the final period of the cosmic cycle—which of the two is irrelevant, since it comes round again and again—living beings come to life, after a long process of monstrous creation and chaos. In any case they are a separation from the Sphairos——the perfect amalgam of all—and their creation is birth. But it is also death in comparison to the perfect peace and contentment of the Sphairos; and when they are reunited into it, they die as separate existences. Correspondingly, the wrenching out of the perfect amalgam of certain elements and their combination into various forms of being is like death; but their dissolution and their return to their "kindred" elements—air to air, fire to fire, etc.—is also death for the individual being. This dispersion does not necessarily result in the perfect amalgamation of all the elements, but may result in a period of disorder and chaos, which Empedocles pictures very vividly and horrifically in another part of his work. Dispersion may therefore mean either the end of the initial union and the beginning of creation, or the death of a particular living being. Human beings do not realize this basic truth. For:

> Many ills penetrate through them into their minds and blunt
> their wits. Having seen in their life only a small part of
> the whole, quick death overtakes them and rising into the air
> they fly away like smoke; being aware only of what each man
> happens to have crossed upon; driven hither and thither, but
>   boasting each
> that they have seen the whole (truth).   (DK, 31B fr. 2)

Thus dispersion of the original unity may mean birth to particular creatures, and the dispersion of their particular combination of elements will mean their death. Again, unity and amalgamation of all the elements will mean death to particular beings, and a fitting combination of certain elements in proper proportions will constitute their birth.

The interpretation of pre-Socratic philosophy by the later commentators is throughout bedeviled by the prevalence of Aristotelian and Platonic notions of essence and attributes; from (ideas) and matter; first cause and the concept of the good, often identified with God or the first cause. Thus the One becomes Necessity and elements are its matter, and Love and Strife (Empedocles' two forces) becoming their forms or prototypes. (Cf. Aetius, *De Placitis Philosophorum*, I, 7.28, in DOX, 303.) Stobaeus falls back on opposing qualities that are really relative—differentiated only in degree—and hence little cited by any of the great pre-Socratics. "The nature of the elements is composed of opposites, hot and cold, dry and humid" says Stobaeus. (CW, I, 35 1.17). One should rid oneself of all such notions to begin to understand Parmenides, Heraclitus, or Empedocles.

Let it be noted that Empedocles speaks of the elements on three levels: (a) when he calls them by name, as earth, fire, air, etc.; (b) when by these same words he means, not the elements proper, but their visible and common counterparts, the earth we tread, the sunlight we see, the air we breathe; (c) in a mythological and symbolic way. It is essential to distinguish between these three meanings to arrive at a clear idea of the significance of any particular fragment.

Thus these four elements—fire, air (incidentally Empedocles often calls the air ether, but they are not two distinct elements), water, and earth—"mix" in various proportions, "running through each other"; and it depends on their mutual proportions what sort of thing or creature will result. When the elements separate again, the creature, as we say, dies but the elements themselves are not destroyed. Either they return to the mass of their homogeneous elements, or they enter into new combinations, producing new beings and mortal creatures. "In addition to these (the elements) there is nothing which either comes into being or perishes and ends. . . . No, they are themselves and, running through each other, they become at times different, yet for ever and ever the same." (DK, 31B fr. 17) Mortal creatures disappear when the elements separate; this is difficult for men to grasp:

> There is no man so wise that he could guess in his mind;
> that while they live—what they call life—
> there happen to them things good and bad. But before
>   (the elements)
> adhered together and after they have separated, they were,
> and are, nothing at all.   (DK, 31B fr. 15)

And:

> From these grow all things that ever were and are and will be:
> Trees, and men and women, and birds and beasts,
> and the fish nourished in salty water,
> as well as the long-lived gods, honored above all.
> For they (the elements) are always themselves, but
> running through each other, they take on various forms and
>   shapes,
> So much does the mixture change them.   (DK, 31B fr. 21)

And the well-known fragment of the painters:

> As when painters, intending to adorn votive offerings,
> men well-versed in their art, knowledgeable by the force of
>   their mind,
> having kneaded many-hued substances in their hands,
> mix them harmoniously, here a little more, there a little less,
> and from these create forms that resemble all things,
> raising up trees and buildings, and men and women,
> wild beasts and birds and fish nurtured in water,
> and even gods, long-lived, honored above all;
> Thus let not deceit mislead thy mind and show thee
> that from elsewhere in the source of all
> mortal things, however many are apparent to sense.
>   (DK, 31B fr. 23)

The Forces. The elements do not seem to Empedocles sufficient to account for the unceasing change of visible things. Change constitutes our world; without it we could not imagine either the world or our own being. He considered the elements as more or less inert in themselves and not the agents of the continuous mingling and separation to which they were subjected. In Empedocles' view, these changes were ordained by two contrasting forces ceaselessly at war with each other. They are Love (other names for which are Amity, Aphrodite, Harmony, Kypris) and Strife or Hatred (Neikos). Their various names add to the poetical atmosphere of his verses and do not lead to confusion, as the mythological name of the elements do. The forces cannot be taken as personal causes directing the world, because they, too, are subject to the law of the cosmic cycle. Strife creates havoc, enmity; and when it infiltrates into the perfectly amalgamated union of all the elements in the Sphairos, Strife produces a vortex-like movement which disperses the elements in all directions. From that dispersion, unnatural shapes and events originate, probably deluges and eruptions of volcanos, floods, and crumbling of mountains. Strife is also the cause of unnatural living creatures, whose description by Empedocles is detailed and horrific—monsters with men's bodies and bovine heads, or the other way around; creatures with a double face, looking both fore and aft; worse still, isolated limbs roaming about, arms without supporting shoulders, eyes without a forehead over them, and many other queer combinations. Some fragments illustrate Empedocles' power of imagination in picturing the horrible as vividly as the harmonious:

> in which many a head grew without a neck, and naked arms
> wandered about without supporting shoulders,
> and eyes bereft of a forehead.   (DK, 31B fr. 57)
> ... (creature) with trailing feet and countless hands ...
>   (DK, 31B, fr. 60)
> Many creatures with faces fore and aft, and breasts both ways;
> oxen with human brows and conversely men with bovine heads
> and creatures mixed male and female, with deep-seated sexual
>   organs.   (DK, 31B fr. 61)

It is probable that in painting these pictures, Empedocles was influenced by mythological representations from Oriental peoples as well as from Greece itself. Archaic Greek art is full of gorgons, harpies, griffons, and other such images. It was not until the end of the 5th century that Greek art gradually emancipated itself from such images, retaining them only as ornamental details on the corners of roofs and such places. They had by then become innocuous. But the very real monsters which populated our earth before man appeared—pterodactyls etc.—remind us that the present species in the world are not the only ones ever created. As part of Empedocles' biology, these creatures represent a stage in physical evolution.

All these were the results of Strife's supremacy. But Amity, or

Harmony was also at work. She (let us use the feminine, as Empedocles does) pushes Strife, or Dissention, away from the centre to the outer edges of the world. But he describes how gradual is the conquest of Amity over Strife, against whose disorders she has to fight her way inch by inch

> From their mixture, thousands
> of mortal creatures poured out, yet still remained unmixed
> while Strife still held hovering aloft.
> For Strife did not at once retreat to the outer edges
> of the circle, but in some limbs still remained fast
> while from others it had already gone.   (DK, 31B fr. 35)

As Strife is pushed aside and made to withdraw to the outer edges of the cosmos;

> As it ran under
> and went away, so far could there enter the pure onrush
> of mild-minded Amity. And all of a sudden
> they became mortal, those previously wont to be immortal,
> and compact those previously unmixed, changing their ways.
> Thus myriads of forms, well-knit together, came into being,
> a wonder to behold.   (DK, 31B fr. 35)*

That Aristotle saw the function of Empedocles' forces in part correctly is shown by his remark intended as adverse criticism: "For, he says, Strife often divides and Amity often separates, while Strife brings together. . . ." (AMP, I. iv. 985a. 25) The two forces are not on the same level as the four elements but can be best understood in the analogy of positive and negative electricity, or as forces of attraction and repulsion acting on the molecules of the elements, conceived as in 19th century physics. Present-day physics makes no distinction between matter and energy, just as

*The word rendered by "compact" gave rise in Alexandrine and Roman times to lively controversy. Plutarch (PQC, v. 4,1, 677D) mentions that Sosicles, the poet, uses the word in the meaning of well-mixed. Although I have accepted the use of the word "compact" in accordance with the most authoritative translations, I suggest very tentatively that the word "zora" may be a poetic shortening of a word still current in modern Greek: "zoera," meaning lively.

Heraclitus did not differentiate fire from the things it consumes.

It is not quite clear whether Empedocles conceived the elements as continuous, homogeneous stuff, which can be melted with another, as water is with earth to make mud. In two fragments he seems to think of them like this, for he introduces examples of tin mixing with copper (DK, 31B fr. 92) and of flax mixing with the "silvery elder's seed." (DK, 31B fr. 82) Part of Empedocles' controversy with the Hippocratean school of medicine centred on this point; that is, on the expression "running through each other." (DK, 31B fr. 17,21,26 et al.) Galen, according to Hipollytus, objected to this view, saying that Hippocrates did not accept, like Empedocles, that the elements ran through each other. (CMG, 19.7) He compares Empedocles' conception to the pounding together of different kinds of stone and metal until they become a kind of paste from which one can no more separate the various ingredients; while Hippocrates held that the molecules of the elements maintained their impermeability, and the mixture consisted in their lying close together, in thick clusters of heterogenous particles. In accepting this criticism, we make Empedocles the forerunner of chemical union, as against the mechanistic view; which may well be right. Aëtius, probably inspired by that criticism, says that Empedocles and Xenophanes both regard the elements as composed of smaller constituent parts which one could call "elements of elements." (DOX, 312, 315) These were essentially of the same quality, undifferentiated from each other (by which he presumably meant that one particle of water is exactly like any other particle of water, the same holding for the particles of earth, air, etc.).

We digress; as already stated, Empedocles held that the forces of Love and Hate alternate in predominating over the world. The tendency of the former was to unite, to make one out of many; and of the latter, to disperse things in all directions, without order or design. Hatred does not simply separate the world into its four constituent elements, which would result in an ordered stratification of the elements, each joining with its own, and leading to complete immobility. Instead, Hatred throws them about without any order, producing in the process monstrous creatures unable to survive. These monstrous creations are slowly eliminated as Amity gains the upper hand at the "appointed time." Appointed by whom, or what? Empedocles seems to believe in an ineluctable, eternal decree of Fate or Necessity, in a supreme Law that is above the elements, above the forces, above the gods. This decree of Fate "bound by the most solemn oaths" is explicitly mentioned in a fragment from his second work, *The Purifications* (DK, 31B fr. 115), but analogous expressions, "when the circle comes round," or "when time returns," and others such, abound in the fragments of the first work, *On Nature*. They seem to show that the alternate ruling of Amity and Strife does not depend on the two forces themselves—"Amity abhors Necessity hard to bear" (DK, 31B fr. 116)—But on another force they are obliged to obey. It cannot be maintained with certainty that Necessity acts mechanically but its actions are certainly not ordained by the gods, who, throughout Empedocles' first work, are "long-lived, honoured above all" but not eternal.

The Sphairos. Each of Empedocles' cosmic cycles has a single supreme period. This is the Sphairos, the apex of perfection, the absolute fulfilment with no distinction of qualities, no separate creatures, no personality, no becoming and decaying. All the elements are merged in the Sphairos in a state of absolute equilibrium. It is immense, equal all around but not limitless, though one fragment calls it "infinite on all sides." The Sphairos can only be negatively defined. It has no limits and no sensation or feeling, unless it be the sense of itself "exultant in surrounding solitude."* It is a supreme achievement of Empedocles' philosophic insight and poetic power that he manages to convey this metaphysical conception as indicating intense satisfaction and giving an impression that it would indeed be a fulfilment to be merged in something like the Sphairos.

The idea of the world as an immensely large but not infinite

---

*The expression "exultant in surrounding solitude" is taken from W.E. Leonard's translation of fragments 27 and 28.

sphere was already current in many philosophical schools. Xenophanes had defined the divine as a sphere, separate yet coexisting
with the perceptible world. Parmenides conceived the world as an
immobile sphere, since for him all movement was a deception of
the senses:

> Since there is an outer limit, it (the One) is completed,
> on all sides, similar in extent, at the same distance from the center.
> It cannot grow either larger or smaller, or this way and that.
>
> (DK, 28B fr. 8)

This world cannot be experienced with the senses: it *is* the world
and it is there all the time. The difference is that, for Empedocles,
the Sphairos represents a stage in the cosmic cycle. It will be
destroyed and re-created again and again:

> In it were not to be seen the swift limbs of the sun
> nor the earth's dense vegetation; nor yet the sea.
> So much was the Sphairos firmly embedded
> within the secret compactness of harmony, spherical all around,
> exultant in surrounding solitude.   (DK, 31B fr. 27)

Again:

> But he, on all sides equal and altogether infinite,
> the rounded Sphairos, exultant in surrounding solitude.
>
> (DK, 31B fr. 28)

A few lines earlier, he gives a negative definition:

> There is no faction or unjust strife in its limbs.
>
> (DK, 31B fr. 27)

Another fragment, shortly after, shows that the expression
"limbs" was wrong:

> From its back no twin branching arms are swinging;
> it has no feet or swift-moving knees, or sexual organ shaggy,
> It is a sphere, on all sides equal unto itself.   (DK, 31B fr. 29)

Meanwhile, the state of mind of mortals is contemptible, puny, unable to conceive what really *is;* a will-of-the-wisp, dependent on the chance agglomeration of some particles of the elements. The contrast to the condition of the Sphairos, which they cannot understand, is expressive of despair, and yet at the same time Empedocles exults, because he alone is able to conceive and accept an understanding of the universe.

Mortals emerge only when the perfect balance of the Sphairos is destroyed by Strife. They are pitiable, short-lived, with dim minds and perceptions, steeped in error. Numerous passages refer to the mortal's miserable lot. Even Empedocles' chosen follower, Pausanias, will be able to learn no more of the things that can be neither seen nor heard than human mind can grasp:

> These things can be neither seen, nor heard, nor conceived
> by the mind. But thou, since thou has wandered hither,
> shalt learn, yet no more than human intellect can reach.
>   (DK, 31B fr. 2)

Since the Sphairos represents the final stage of each cosmic cycle (which also constitutes the initial phase of the following one) personal immortality is out of the question. One fragment explicitly denies survival after death or existence before birth:

> But before (the elements)
> adhered together, and after they have separated, they were,
> and are, nothing at all.   (DK, 31B fr. 15)

Men are on a par with all other creatures. They have neither a distinctive "soul" nor immortality. Their thoughts depend on what they happen to have encountered. They rejoice or grieve over the coming together or the separation of the elements. They call these things birth and death. Even I, says Empedocles, talk like that by force of usage.

> When, having come together in the proper mixture (the
>   elements)
> they rise to the light in the shape of a man, or as beasts living
>   in the wild
> or as bushes or birds, the people call it birth and creation;

and when they separate, they call it ill-fated death.
I, too, talk like that, by force of usage.   (DK, 31B fr. 9)

Empedocles seems to have forestalled Aristotle's objection in
the passage of the *Metaphysics* referred to above, that it was not
only Strife that separated but also Amity, and that sometimes
Strife joins things together. For to form a harmonious whole,
Amity has sometimes to reject—hence to dissolve—certain combinations; and again Strife does join things together, though in a
disorderly way. That is why, in a decisive fragment, whose first
lines have already been quoted, Empedocles states:

Double is the birth of mortal things and double their demise.
For the coming together of all both causes their birth
and destroys them; and separation nurtured in their being
makes them fly apart. These things never stop changing
throughout; at times coming together through Amity in one
    whole,
at other times being violently separated by Strife.
Thus, on one side one whole is formed out of many
and then again, wrenched from one another, they make up many
    out of one.
Thus they come into being and their life is not long their own.
                                                    (DK, 31B fr. 17)

In another verse of the same fragment, Empedocles returns to the
subject:

I shall speak a double truth: at times one has grown out of many,
at other times many grow apart out of the one,
fire and water and earth and the immeasurable heights of air.
Then dire Strife stands away from all, while Love
reigns in their midst, equal in length and breadth.
Do thou look (at these things) with thy mind, and don't sit there
gaping in amazement at what thine eyes show thee.
Love by the mortals is considered innate and harmonious,
and those well-disposed towards her perform fine works
and call her Bliss and Aphrodite. But no mortal man
has seen her wending her way among the elements . . .
These are all equal one to the other and of the same age . . .
They are forever themselves, but running

through each other they become at times different
yet are for ever and ever the same.   (DK, 31B fr. 17)

In another fragment, Empedocles returns again to the same
subject, with more emphasis on the immortality of the elements:

From these grow all things that ever were and are and will be:
Trees, and men and women, and birds and beasts,
and the fish nourished in salty water,
as well as the long-lived gods, honoured above all.
For they (the elements) are always themselves, but
running through each other, they take on various forms and
    shapes,
so much does the mixture change them.   (DK, 31B fr. 21)

The Process. It was hinted already that the coming together
and separation of the elements is subjected to a universal law,
"stretched overall" and held fast by a "wide oath." Various inter-
pretations have been put forward as to the sequence of this
process, hence as to the phases through which the world must
periodically pass before returning—after incalculable stretches of
time—to the same condition. L. N. Boussoulas has devoted many
monographs to Empedocles' "mixture," some of them published
in the well-known French review of philosophy, "Revue de Métaphysique et de Morale." However, I cannot agree with his conclusions, which contradict express statements in the poetry of
Empedocles.

Empedocles is aware that each of the two forces simultaneously
unites and separates elements or groups of elements. Therefore,
the process cannot have a simple and easily understandable meaning; for Strife both separates and unites, and Amity acts likewise.
It is the *nature* of what results when they mix the elements together or separate them apart that is different. Amity creates
myriads of living creatures, differing in shape and colour. Strife
creates monstrosities and non-viable beings. But it does this by
tearing elements away from the state in which they were before—
separation—as well as by coalescing other groups of elements.
Empedocles is conscious this may create difficulties in the mind

of the reader—or hearer—and that is why he repeats in many fragments, using many different expressions: ". . . if any of that which
I have said is deficient, let me repeat how each thing came to
be . . ."

The composition of the universe out of the four elements and
their various mixtures, as Empedocles conceived it, may now be
relatively clear. But the process by which Empedocles thought
mortal beings—from the amoeba to the stars and the gods—originate and return to their doom must now be discussed.

The process was circular, each cycle covering an immense
stretch of time. Perhaps the cycles corresponded to the Babylonian "long year," two minutes of which are equivalent to one
earthly year. Hence one of its days is the equivalent of 720 earthly
years, and one of its years as long as 262,800 of our years.

As the cosmic process is a cycle, it is irrelevant at which point
we begin. This thought is also expressed by Parmenides: "It is all
the same to me where I should begin; for that point I shall again
at some time reach"; (DK, 28B fr. 5) and Heraclitus: "For the
beginning and the end coincide on the circumference of a circle";
(DK, 22B fr. 103) and Empedocles: "Since they undergo these
changes in a certain order, it can be said that they are immobile
in a circle." (I paraphrase a fragment already quoted, and which
we shall encounter again repeatedly.)

Let us therefore begin with the Sphairos. We have seen that this
notion is not absolutely original, since both Xenophanes and Parmenides talk of a sphere. Xenophanes identifies the Sphere with
the divine, which adopts this shape to make its difference from
the anthropomorphic gods as great as possible. Xenophanes'
Sphere is all-seeing and all-hearing and all-thinking, but it does not
breathe. It is transcendent, existing at the same time as the visible
world. It is a conception that Xenophanes reveres, so far as he
reveres anything. Parmenides' Sphere *is* the world; the One, the
Whole. It is immobile—a plenum; and any changes in quality or
any movement that we may notice is a deception of the senses—
"opinion" (doxa), not "truth." Empedocles' Sphairos is like
neither of these conceptions. It does not exist all the time, it is
one of the four salient phases in the cosmic process.

In the Sphairos of Empedocles, all the elements, the whole contents of the world, are merged together; there is nothing outside it. This perfect amalgam constitutes an equally perfect harmony, inaccessible to any sensation or thought. While the Sphairos lasts, there are neither men, nor beasts, nor the shaggy strength of the wooded earth; nor even gods. The gods, it is true, live longer than the creatures, presumably covering one or more of the four cosmic periods; but they also are absorbed into the Sphairos. In it, all consciousness of joy or pain is absent. One could say consciousness is altogether absent but for the expression that the Sphairos is "exultant in surrounding solitude." We do not know whether Empedocles realized that, by this expression, he posited the void—which the Eleatics denied and which he himself had been at pains to refute. The Sphairos therefore is a condition or unconscious bliss, or perfect unity, with neither movement nor becoming, and no sun, earth, gods, or living creatures to disturb its ineffable peace. We must also imagine it as very compact, since it contains all the matter that exists. One school of modern astronomy supposes that the world was produced by a terrific explosion of an immensely compact and comparatively small conglomeration of atoms.

It is significant of the poetic force of Empedocles that, even on such an abstract concept, he manages to convey a feeling that the Sphairos is a state of supreme fulfilment and that it would be a worthy culmination to be merged in such a perfect, ineffable peace, compared to which individual lives are passing incidents, not worth preserving as such. Let us turn again to some of the expressions Empedocles uses to describe the Sphairos:

> In it were not to be seen the swift limbs of the sun,
> nor the earth's dense vegetation; nor yet the sea.
> So much was the Sphairos firmly embedded
> within the secret compactness of Harmony,
> spherical all round, exultant in surrounding solitude.
>
> (DK, 31B fr. 27)

The horror of the unlimited, inherited from both Parmenides and the Pythagoreans, prevails in all but one of the fragments. Only in one does Empedocles call the Sphairos limitless, though still attributing to it the rounded shape, on all sides equal to itself. It is only natural that in the course of composing such a long epic poem, a contradiction may crop up now and then. However, even if the Sphairos was limited, the "surrounding solitude" might not be so.

Then "at the appointed time" this ineffable peace is disturbed by the start of an inner movement somewhat like a vortex. Strife has managed to penetrate into the Sphairos and "one by one the limbs of the god started shaking." Here of course Empedocles is carried away by his poetic bent; for the Sphairos has no limbs, but only undifferentiated parts. Strife gradually gains the upper hand, and begins scattering the parts of the Sphairos in all directions. He does not disperse them according to their kind—earth to one side, water to another, and so on for air and fire—as he would then achieve a stratification containing no principle of change. Strife simply scatters the elements randomly, so that they enter into haphazard combinations with one another. It is a disordered chaos, a havoc, from which monstrosities originate, as we have already related. Nevertheless, it cannot be said that Strife's work is merely dispersion; it is also a process of union, though of heterocline elements. This is the basis of Empedocles' insistence on the "double truth," which he is going to proclaim. Again and again he opens with the words: "I shall tell a double truth."

After a long period of utter confusion, Amity finds her way into the center of the world and begins pushing Strife to the outer edges. Thus begins the third period of the cycle. It is the period during which Amity reigns supreme, after the "myriads of living creatures have poured out of her loving hands." Descriptions of this period abound in both works of Empedocles, *On Nature* as well as *Purifications*. If the Sphairos was the apogee of Harmony and coalescence of all things into one, we may call the period of Amity's reign the "perigee." She moulds everything in her "impecable palms," she leads "the throng of mute fish spawning abundantly"; all creatures in this era are tame and friendly towards each other and toward man. No gods of war—Zeus, Ares (Mars) or Poseidon—yet exist, but only Kypris or Aphrodite (Amity). Empedocles returns again and again with true inspiration to that long-lost age. The two following fragments, incomplete in that the main clause is missing, attempts to explain how Amity fashioned so many different creatures from the bare four elements:

> If explanation of these things seems to thee somewhat deficient,
> and thou wonderest how, from earth and water and air,
> and the sun's fire, being mixed, so many mortal kinds of creatures
> of so many colours, as now enjoy life, fitted together by
>   Aphrodite . . .   (DK, 31B fr. 71)

And the next, probably a sequence of the previous one:

> As then Kypris made earth soft by sprinkling it with water,
> gave all species to swift fire to strengthen them . . .
>   (DK, 31B fr. 73)

In that age trees had foliage and produced plenty of fruit all the year round, raising their branches aloft into the air. These fragments are from *On Nature*. In the *Purifications* Empedocles describes how the people of that age worshipped Kypris or Amity:

> Nor Zeus the King, or Kronos or Poseidon;
> but Kypris was the queen.
> They worshipped and conciliated her with pious delights,
> with painted semblances of animals and sweet-smelling burnt
>   incense,
> whose clouds of scented smoke made all sorts of patterns in
>   the air,
> with myrrh and bloodless herbs burning. On the floor,
> before her altar they made libations of blonde honey. Her altars
> were never smeared by the blood of bulls, for this was considered
> a heinous crime among men, to wet their own limbs
> with the pure red gushing blood, having torn the life out of
>   the beast.   (DK, 31B fr. 128)

It is not preposterous to suggest that this picture of a paradise-like world presents an historical memory—already hallowed by time and tradition—of a civilization totally different from that of

the Greeks of Empedocles' time: the Aegean, or Minoan, pre-
Greek civilization, which prevailed over the greater part of the
Mediterranean basin before the descent of the Aryan Greeks from
the North. Its memories lived on among those whom the Greeks
called Eteocretans, and probably also among the Sikels, the pre-
Greek inhabitants of Sicily, who were driven to the remoter
regions of northwest Sicily, as the Welsh were driven by the
Saxons to the western mountainous regions of Britain. The
excavations in Crete show us a highly developed culture, and in
all the frescoes and vase decoration there is no scene of war.
Shields were used as decorative designs; the altars were tiny,
established in the ante-chamber to the throne-room, and it would
have been impossible to perform sacrifices of beasts there. If the
Cretans occasionally waged wars—for example, against pirates in
the islands—they did not glorify war nor combat between men
with spears and shields.

Even as late as in the times of the Neoplatonists (4th-5th cent.
A.D.) Porphyry's *De abstinentia*, relying on Theophrastus' *De
pietate* (II, 2), mentions bloodless sacrifices, and connects Empedocles with the rites of the Corybantes in Crete. In historical
times, the Corybantes performed orgiastic rites, and such orgies
may well have been practiced during certain ceremonies in honor
of the Mother Goddess. But the essence of the beliefs held by the
Cretans, as far as we can judge from the archaeological remains,
were of the character described in Empedocles' verses. The pre-
Greek civilization did not show that preoccupation with war
which distinguished the Greeks.

The over-flourishing and constantly fruit-bearing trees remind
one of the miraculous garden of the Phaeacians, at whose island
Odysseus landed shipwrecked (*Odyssey* VIII). It is clear that the
civilization described in that book was alien to the Greek world:
the dominant position of the queen, Arete, the freedom of movement of the princess, Nausicaa, and her attendants. Also the vagueness of the geographical location, and the fact that the goddess
Athena had plunged Odysseus into a deep sleep during the
voyage, so he could not see the course the ship took and the ship
was then turned into stone, so its course could not be described

on his return to his own country, gives the picture a mythical aspect and symbolizes the complete separation of this pre-Greek survival of a happy, prosperous, and peaceful island, clinging to its traditional civilization from the Aryan world of wars, conquests, and bloodthirsty deeds.

We have seen in the first chapter that Gela, hence also its colony, Akragas, was colonized by two men from different islands, Crete and Rhodes. Both these places had been prominent centers of the Aegean civilization. Though conquered some centuries earlier by the Dorians, they must have kept alive the memory of their past glory and happy peace. This memory—appearing also, though in a debased form, in the tales and songs of the Sikels—may well have inspired Empedocles to identify the perigee of Love with that mythical golden age.

We have described what blessings the almost complete reign of Amity brings to the world: harmonious beings, all tame and friendly to each other, in an endless variety of shapes and colors. The purely biological ideas and problems raised by Empedocles' conception of the development of living creatures will be discussed at greater length in the chapter on his biology. Some scholars have seen in it a foreshadowing of Darwinism: many of Empedocles' observations are extremely acute and betoken considerable knowledge of anatomy.

What interests us in the present context is his overall picture of the stages of the cosmic cycle. Never "blamelessly" (that is, completely and perfectly) does Amity conquer the existing world; Strife still hovers on the outer edges of the universe, ready to reenter it when the opportunity presents itself. By the period in which Empedocles lived, the era of earthly bliss was situated in an already mythical past age. Strife has regained the upper hand, though it does not yet produce monsters, nor play havoc with unnatural combinations of elements. But Strife has firmly established itself in the hearts and minds of men. The gods that "were not yet" in the perigee of Amity, are all now seated in Olympus, intriguing, egging men on to wars and demanding bloody sacrifices. Hatred, destruction of animal species and of each other, perjury and internecine wars plague the human kind.

After Empedocles' conversion to the Pythagorean doctrine of the transmigration of the soul, he becomes deeply conscious of the imbalance in the world. The signs are not yet apparent to all, but they are ominous. Two transgressions against the general law, "stretched all over the universe," guaranteed by the "most solemn oaths" (we do not know who swore them) are rampant among mankind: perjury, and the slaughter of animals in honor of the gods. Amity can do nothing against these transgressions, though "she loathes Necessity, hard to bear." (DK, 31B fr. 116) The gods, whom men worship, do not take any notice of these transgression; indeed they demand the bloody sacrifices, although the bull or cow sacrificed may be a human being changed in form—even may be the father, son, or mother of the sacrificer. The world has bcome a dismal place, on entering which man "weeps and wails." (DK, 31B fr. 118) In his description of the primeval monsters of the second period, Empedocles can be considered dispassionate and distant. It is otherwise with the horror he feels for animal sacrifices. In the reign of Amity:

> For it was considered a heinous crime among men, to wet their
>   own limbs
> with the pure red gushing blood, having torn the life out of
>   the beast.   (DK, 31B fr. 128)

Heraclitus was also strongly against animal sacrifices, but he viewed it from further off and stretched the irrationality of it: "They atone for bloodshedding," he says, "by snearing themselves with blood, as if to clease oneself from mud, you had to wallow in mud." (DK, 22B fr. 6) But Empedocles addresses passionate appeals to his fellow-men:

> Will you not stop this norsome awful slaughter? Do you not see
> how you tear each other to pieces in the blindness of your mind?
>   (DK, 31B fr. 136)

And:

> The father, the utter fool, lifting his knife slits the throat
> of his own dear son, who has changed his form; and the
>   bystanders

offer prayers while he sacrifices. He, mindless of the entreaties
of the poor victim, having killed him prepares in his princely
halls a horrible meal. In the same way, a son catches and kills
his mother; children, their father; and having torn the life
out of them, they consume their kindred flesh.

(DK, 31B fr. 137)

In the "joyless place" that the world has now become, "murder
and wrath, and myriads of other small banes and shrivelling
diseases and rottenness and works without result run away like
water. All these wander about in the dark in the fields of the
Avenging Power." (DK, 31B fr. 121)*

In the following two fragments, Empedocles lets himself go in
describing the various "banes." (DK, 31B fr. 122,123) Most of the
names are his own inventions and the adjectives he appends to
them are often original, though they do not convey any reason
why one particular bane should have a particular attribute. For
example, why should Vagueness be black-haired or Harmony
grey-eyed? These banes go in pairs, one good and the other bad,
Beauty and Ugliness, Silence and Talk, etc. The whole enumeration is a series of verbal fireworks that may have made the crowds
at Olympia gape in amazement, especially if recited quickly, but
the list adds nothing either to Empedocles' poetry, or to the
understanding of his underlying vision. However, it is obvious
by his description of the world as a dismal, or a joyless place—
a roofed-over cave where all these small demons persecute mankind like noxious insects—with murder, wrath, perjury, etc. rampant, that Empedocles refers to the period in the cosmic cycle
presaging the return of Strife in all its might. What form its new

---

*The expression which I rendered in a somewhat prolix way, by "works
without result, running away like water" is contained in only two words of
Empedocles. These two words, which are understood by any Greek (even
though he might not know ancient Greek), are translated by Leonard as
"Labors, burdened with the water-jars," probably thinking of the Danaids
who draw water externally in cracked jars, which always reach their destina-
tion empty. Still worse is the translation of Diels-Kranz, who render the
expression by "das Wirken des Rheuma" which does not make sense in any
language.

prevalence will take, we cannot guess. Certainly it cannot resemble the first onslaught of Strife when it disturbed the Sphairos, since Strife has not now got the raw material, so to say, of an undifferentiated amalgam of the elements. Strife cannot again create the terrible monstrous creatures it did in that period, but it can undermine what remains of harmony, peace, and beauty in living beings: it can make them destroy each other, or die of shrivelling diseases and pain.

Strife had not yet reached its full stature in Empedocles' time; nor has it yet in ours. For, measured in terms of the cosmic cycle or of the Babylonian long years, our time is not very distant from that of Empedocles.

Empedocles does not indulge in prophecies of what will happen next—which may be an indirect proof that the basis of his description of the reign of Amity was historical. After Strife finally again gains absolutely the upper hand, what then? When we reach this point in Empedocles' cycle, we come up against a blank. Since there are only four stages of the cosmic cycle, it seems we must expect the restoration of the Sphairos. This might come about in one of two ways: Amity might again intervene and restore the "perigee" of her reign; but this would preclude the advent of the Sphairos, and we should have only two alternative periods of worldly life, presided over in turn by Strife and Amity. The alternative is the sudden wiping out of all creation, and a return to the primeval condition of absolute unity, peace, and beauty. We cannot be certain what Empedocles' thought was on this matter, but there are hints in the fragments we shall presently quote, that it is the force of Amity which reproduces the Sphairos. Therefore on the accompanying design of the four cycles, the period following the second prevalence of Strife is marked only with the dotted line of doubt. (See diagram, p. 72.)

We can say however that we are more or less certain of the first two stages of Empedocles' cosmic cycle, and that we have intimations of the beginning of the third. It seems that the Sphairos and the reign of Kypris—the two points A and C on the diagram— for a time at least, are more or less static. The first, the Sphairos, does not seem to contain in itself the seeds of its own destruction.

But the other that we called the "perigee of Amity" may be said to include them. Even though this period was an early paradise, death was certain for all, and the human race was no more advanced in knowledge and wisdom than at the present day. Empedocles postulates no great intellectual power for men in that period. Though they act rightly and live at peace with creation they are still without sense, driven hither and thither by what they happen to come across, unable to conceive what can neither be seen nor heard, and destined to fly away like smoke when the elements composing their body separate. They acted rightly then, but they might easily have been influenced to do the opposite, as they did in Empedocles' time. We can only hint at the problem of whether the new rise of Hatred is brought about partly or wholly by human agency? The passionate exhortations of Empedocles against bloody sacrifice seem to indicate that men can influence the development of their society. The second and third phase of the cosmic cycle, after the bursting apart of the Sphairos, cannot be attributed to man. In the first he did not yet exist and he was still very imperfect while Amity strove for him. Both these phases took place *in time;* and the fourth phase—the time of Empedocles—is gradually evolving. Thus all the changes of the cosmic cycle have been, and are, taking place in time. We have seen that Love gained ground from Strife painfully and painstakingly and far from suddenly, and all the fragments quoted seem to show that the deterioration which both we and Empedocles witness is also gradual. Only the last stroke—its complete destruction—may come suddenly, for we cannot conceive the gradual increase of Strife as leading to the Sphairos. And because we cannot imagine how the process can lead to this conclusion, we may surmise its sudden advent. It is this inner contradiction—not a trivial philological "analysis," taking one word from here and connecting it with another single word there—that leads us to conceive it was not impossible for there to be a sudden change from the welter into which Strife is leading us to the ineffable peace and balance of the Sphairos. It would be as if Necessity, or whatever presides over the cosmic cycle, decided to scrap the whole of the world, which was falling into decay and disorder, and to merge the elements into their perfect equilibrium, until the time came round again to start once more, with the same hopeless prospect.

The existing fragments of Empedocles' work *On Nature* do not open any prospect or hope of getting out of the cycle, of fighting mortality, obscurantism, limitation. Nor does he seem to grieve over it. He thought the aeons would always succeed each other, bringing with them periods of the ineffable bliss of the lonely Sphairos, then the monsters and the cataclysms, succeeded by the world as it pours out of the loving palms of Aphrodite. Lastly the gradual return of Hatred, the period in which he lived. In whichever period a mortal happened to be born, he would have the mentality of that age, and find it natural either to fight or to live in concord with the other creatures. In either case, the particular combination of elements which formed that creature would be bound to dissolve, and it would be no more, flying away like smoke. Only rare individuals, like Pythagoras, Heraclitus, and himself, were able to survey the whole of the process.

On Nature does not offer any ethical scale of values, nor give any moral advice. The forces, he tells us, have always existed and will always alternate with each other:

> As the two were of old, so they'll always be, nor ever, I think,
> will immeasurable time be emptied of them both.
>
> (DK, 31B fr. 16)

And

> These are all equal one to the other and of the same age, but each
>   is honored
> differently and has its special destiny to perform,
> and they predominate in turn as the circle comes round.
>
> (DK, 31B, fr 17)*

This imaginary reconstruction of the process may enable the reader to undrstand more easily Empedocles' statement about the

---

*There is a problem here; what are those "all." Diels-Kranz interprets them as both the elements and the forces, and the use of the world 'all" seems to justify this conception; yet we have not heard of *the elements* predominating alternately, nor of their enjoying any honors.

"double truth," which recurs again and again, showing that the author himself was aware of the difficulties he had raised.

I shall speak a double truth; at times
one alone comes into being;
at other times out of one several things grow.
Double is the birth of mortal things and double their demise.
For the coming together of all both causes their birth
and destroys them; and separation nurtured in their being
makes them fly apart. These things never stop changing
throughout, at times coming together through Amity in one
    whole,
at other times being violently separated by Strife.
Thus, on one side, one whole is formed out of many,
and then again, wrenched from each other, they make up many
    out of one.
Thus they come into being and their life is not long their own,
but insofar as they never stop changing throughout
insofar they are forever immovable in a circle.
But come, listen to my words, for knowledge makes the
    mind grow.
As I said once before, revealing the outer limits of my thought,
I shall speak a double truth; at times one has grown out of many,
at other times many grow apart out of the one,
fire and water and earth and the immeasurable heights of air.
Then dire Strife stands away from all, while Love
reigns in their midst, equal in length and breadth.
Do thou look (at these things) with thy mind, and don't sit there
gaping in amazement at what thine eyes show thee.
Love by the mortals is considered innate and harmonious,
and those well-disposed towards her perform fine works
and call her Bliss and Aphrodite. But no mortal man
has seen her wending her way among the elements.
Yet thou must listen to words not deceptively put together.
These are all equal one to the other and of the same age.
But each is honored differently and has its special destiny to
    perform
and they predominate in turn as the circle comes round.
In addition to these there is nothing which either comes
into being or perishes and ends . . . For if they perished totally
they would not be at all. Or else what would there be

> to make the Whole greater? Whence would it come?
> No, they (the elements) are forever themselves, but running
> through each other they become at times different
> yet are for ever and ever the same. (DK, 31B fr. 17)

I think one should interpret the word "these" in "these are all equal one to the other" as meaning the two forces, but three lines later, "in addition to these, there is nothing" must mean the elements, in addition to which there is nothing real.

Empedocles is conscious that, despite all he has said, the process has not been understood by his sole disciple. Hence, he repeats in it in a slightly different form in another fragment, and probably there were several other repetitions in other parts of his work. It is this that probably made Aristotle say disparagingly that Empedocles continually repeats himself and yet thinks he is saying something new every time.

> I shall now retrace my steps and come back to my song's beginning,
> to what I said before, letting new words flow
> from those I previously uttered. When namely Strife
> stood at the lowest depth of the whirl and Amity was established
> in its midst, all these came together into one;
> not far from each other but thickly close together,
> coming from different directions. From their mixture, thousands
> of mortal creatures poured out, yet still remained unmixed
> while Strife still held hovering aloft.
> For Strife did not at once retreat to the outer edges
> of the circle, but in some limbs still remained fast
> while from others it had already gone. As it ran under
> and went away, in-so-far could there enter the pure onrush
> of mild-minded Amity. And all of a sudden
> they became mortal, those previously wont to be immortal,
> and compact those previously unmixed, changing their ways.
> Thus myriads of forms, well-knit together, came into being,
> a wonder to behold. (DK, 31B fr. 35)

The expression "all of a sudden" seems to contradict the gradual taking over of the world by Amity, though this is clearly indicated in the two preceding verses. The statement can, however, be reconciled if we interpret it to mean that the sudden change came for each creature separately, as birth is a sudden event, though prepared a long time before; so as Strife ran under and went away, in so far could there enter the pure onrush of Aphrodite.

In interpreting the elements and the process, I have disregarded the numerous comments of the ancients on this crucial point of Empedocles' theory, for they are full of misunderstandings. For example, Aristotle repeatedly expresses his horror at those philosophers who think the heavens were created: "Anaxagoras made the world come into being once, Empedocles many times." (AMP, I. iii 984a; AC 279b 17; *et al.*) We have already noted that he at one place seems to imply that Empedocles' elements were not really four, but two, contrasting air, water, and earth, which he lumps together as one matter, and fire. (AGC, 330 b 20) Aristotle also considers the forces as on the same level and of the same quality as the elements. Simplicius maintains that there were three books of the work *On Nature*, and he allots the fragments to one or the other of them. (DOX, 476) The third book does not seem to have existed at all, or else the second was subdivided by later editions. Many other commentators refer to Empedocles' cosmic theory, but their opinions are vitiated either by the influence of Aristotle's disparaging comments or by later mystical, religious, or other preconceptions. Thus, Diogenes Laertius, though devoting many pages to Empedocles, refers only very briefly to his cosmic theory. (DL, VIII 51–77) Plutarch refers to this theory in many of his works (for example, PQC, V. 4, 1, 677D); and, quoting Hippobotus and Philoponos, he misconstrues the word I have already commented upon: "these" (things), which refers once to the forces, the second time to the elements. Many others— Aetius (DOX, 303, 312–15) and Stobaeus (CW, I, 35 1.17) as well as Galen—also comment on this part of Empedocles' theory. We must stress once again that most of their comments are frequently warped by the preconceptions of their era or are careless and superficial, carrying much less conviction than the force which Empedocles' own thoughts are expressed.

Recapitulation. In sum, there are three main tenets in Empedocles' view of reality:

1. The source of all things is the elements, eternal, changing neither in quality nor in quantity, but *seeming* to change when they mix with each other in different proportions. Properly speaking, the infinite varieties of living things are only an appearance; "their life is not long their own" and they fly away like smoke. But while they exist—"what they call life"—they experience grief and delight, and think they know about their surrounding world. That knowledge and that thought are produced by sensation.

2. The kind, form, and variety of all creatures is determined by the alternate supremacy of the two forces, Amity and Strife, or Love and Hate. They predominate in turn, but they do not seem to have the power of extending or shortening their reign. What presides over their alternate supremacy is an undefined "eternal and ineluctable" law, which is never named but which is hinted at by such expressions as "in the appropriate time" or "when the appropriate time comes round."

3. This process is a cycle of very long duration, repeated ad infinitum; its apex is the Sphairos, when the amalgam of all elements and all their apparent qualities is perfect, when there is no differentiation whatever; and when the Sphairos, comprising all the stuff of the world, rests in ineffable bliss, alone, complete, in total harmony with itself. If we think of the process as a circle, we have a pale reflection of this harmony and happiness in the absolute reign of Amity at the other end of the diameter starting from the Sphairos.

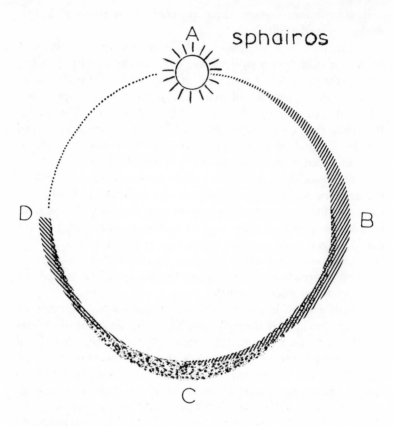

strife

amity

A	The Sphairos.
A-B	Strife enters Sphairos and creates havoc.
B-C	Amity gains gradually the upper hand.
C	Amity reigns supreme.
C-D	Amity retreats before new onslaught of Strife.
D-A	Unknown process and return to Sphairos.

5. SENSATION AND KNOWLEDGE

Although both the theory of the four elements and the notion that the world is periodically destroyed and reborn were current in Empedocles' time, the way in which he envisaged them is original and exclusively his own.

Sensation. Empedocles believed knowledge to be conveyed to the human mind primarily by sensation. His theory of sensation is among the most interesting parts of his doctrine and, if rightly interpreted, can be seen to agree with modern conceptions. We shall take it in isolation, for at some points it clashes with other views of his on the more complicated and abstract processes of thought.

According to Empedocles all things have emanations—effluvia—consisting of small particles of matter, imperceptible in themselves. These produce sensation by striking the appropriate sense-organs which are perforated by equally invisible "passages." One fragment tells us explicitly "For know that there are emanations from all things ever created." (DK 31 B fr. 89). These sense-organ passages respond to different effluvia according to their nature and their size. The first fragment we possess of the work *On Nature* begins: "Narrow passages, instruments of sensation, are scattered all over a man's body." It continues:

Many ills penetrate through them into their minds and blunt their wits. Having seen in their life only a small part of the whole, quick death overtakes them and rising into the air they fly away,

73

like smoke, being aware only of what each man happens to have
come across, driven hither and thither, but boasting each that
they have seen the whole (truth). These things can neither be
seen, nor heard by men, nor conceived by the mind.

(DK 31B fr. 2)

This passage, which is a short summary of Empedocles' whole
theory of sensation, could not in fact have stood at the beginning
of the work, as the expression "these" shows. What are "these"
things? That there are millions of narrow passages perforating the
whole body? If so, why can this fact not be conceived by the
mind? I cannot accept this, for we shall see that Empedocles had
practiced anatomy (perhaps even autopsies of women who died
during pregnancy) and I consider it unlikely that "these things"
refer to the narrow passages which, even if invisible, present no
difficulty to being conceived by the mind; thus, since the ancient
commentators chose their quotations according to the point they
wished to make, paying little heed to the coherence of the whole
theory, I incline to the view that "these things" actually refer to
Empedocles' whole conception of knowledge, which does contain
parts "impossible to conceive for the mind." In other words,
I think that fragment has been assembled by a commentator, and
that its parts do not belong together.

The passages scattered all over the body are of various sizes and
function. Some let through sensations, others the air which regu-
lates the breathing in and out. What one kind of sense-organ can
receive through its passages, leaves the other sense-organs unaffec-
ted; for example, auditory stimuli do not affect the eye; nor does
sight produce any sensation of sound, nor smell any sound or
sight, and so on. This is called today the specific sensibility of each
sense-organ.

What enters through the passages? Empedocles says that everything in existence emits emanations or effluvia of different kinds.
It is these effluvia which, on entering the sense-organs, produce
the sensation. The best instance of how the effluvia affect a sense-
organ is given in two lines: a hound is following the trail of a
beast:

searching with his nostrils the tiny particles of its limbs
left by the wild beast along the tender grass.   (DK 31B fr. 101)

There is a hypothetical supplement to these lines: the words "when alive" were added to make the meter fit (referring to the wild beast). These two words, themselves hypothetical, gave rise to endless discussions among the ancient commentators. Xenophon, who practiced hunting extensively, having even written a small treatise on it, comments that it was impossible for the hound to distinguish the smell of a live beast from that of a dead one and also asks how the hounds discriminate between the smells of the wild beast and other smells; for example, of the grass. Both these objections are ludicrous, and must make us wary of accepting uncritically the remarks of later authors. Theophrastus, who, in his *De Sensu*, discusses at length Empedocles' theory of sensation, finds fault, under the influence of Aristotle, with precisely the original and fundamental part of it, which is based on fact. (DOX, p. 499 ff.)

Smell, as exemplified by the above two lines, may be taken as the archetype of Empedocles' theory of sensation. Something— here particles of matter—enters the sense-organ and affects the nerve-ends spread thickly inside of it—today we might refer to electro-magnetic waves, pulsations of air, and so on. These are stimuli originating from an object but which bear no resemblance to the object itself, and which (by a mechanism still unknown to us today) recreate the object in the mind, or brain, of the recipient. Empedocles knew that different stimuli affect different sense-organs; that is, he foreshadowed what we now call the "specific" function of the sense-organs. "But," says Theophrastus, "the various sensations cannot distinguish (the stimuli) one from the other." Empedocles explains the difference between the various sensations by the size and constitution of the "passages." If these are too large, the stimulus passes through them without affecting them. If they are too small, the stimulus cannot enter at all. This explanation is naive, but it does attempt to account for the fact that each sense-organ only responds to certain kinds of stimuli. However, Aristotle's criticism is even more naive and ignorant; for, on the matter of the particles entering through the nose of the hound, Aristotle says: "If it were so, the smelling substances would be exhausted faster than others." (AGC, 8, 324b, 26) This is, in fact, an easily verifiable phenomenon, but when Aristotle begins a remark with "it is not reasonable" or "it is not likely," he simply means that it is not apparent to the common man's rudimentary sense of logic. Theophrastus however put his finger on an apparent weakness in Empedocles' theory of sensation: that he tries to explain *all* sensation in the same way. But this is both a weakness and a strength; for Empedocles tries to subsume all sensation under the same principle of external stimuli bringing us news of the external world through appropriate entrances spread all over the body: sight, hearing, smell, taste. He explains taste realistically by saying that the tongue, being soft and warm, dissolves the substances coming in touch with it; which is quite right. A view current in Empedocles' time was that the eye not only receives light but emits light as well. In one of the most beautiful of the existing fragments, Empedocles compares the structure of the eye to a lantern, and points out that the sides of the lantern (probably of thin plates of horn), like the "fine veils" that surround the pupil of the eye, prevent wind and rain from penetrating inside, but do not prevent either the lantern or the eye from radiating light from inside outwards, inasmuch as they (the light-rays) are "more fine and thin." Here is the whole of the fragment, which shows, among other things, a detailed knowledge of the anatomy of the eye.

> As when a man, intending to set forth in the wintry night,
> prepares himself a lantern, lighting a flame of burning fire
> whose sides hinder the rush of all winds and scatter their breath,
> while the fire penetrates outside, far as it is finer and more
> tenuous,
> and shines towards the plain with its untiring rays;
> In like fashion was the eternal fire fenced around and hidden
> in finest veils enclosing the round pupil, the veils being
> pierced all over by passages divinely wrought,
> which keep off the watery depths all around
> but let the light through to dart outside, it being more fine
> and thin.   (DK 31B fr. 84)

Another element of his theory is contained in that fragment, which is repeated elsewhere: that we sense like by like, that we see the light by the light inherent in our eyes. This was a common belief in ancient thought, based on the fact that the eye is the only organ of the body which can be seen in absolute darkness. This idea is expressed more clearly, and extended to all the elements in another fragment (DK, 31B fr. 109) and even to the forces in addition to the element.

Most interesting, from the scientific point of view, is Theophrast's remark that Empedocles thought there were in the eye, closely side by side, alternate passages of fire and water, the fire perceiving white, the water black. This is almost an anticipation of the presence in the retina of rods and cones, of which the rods enable us to perceive light and shade and the cones the various colors. Empedocles also sought to explain why some animals see better in the dark. He thought in their eyes the fire was much greater; and that the bright light of day hemmed their own light in, but that it could easily radiate outward during the night. This explanation, though wrong, show how attentive to detail was his curiosity about external phenomena. In his view, the best sighted creatures are those with an exactly balanced mixture of fire and water; excess in either produces defects.

The eyes, both as a sense organ and as an object, seem to have moved Empedocles deeply. Amity fashioned them with particular care, as is shown in several fragments:

> The gentle flame (of the eyes) got only a small part of earth.
> (DK 31B fr. 85)
> From which divine Aphrodite formed solid our untiring eyes
> (DK 31B fr. 86)
> Aphrodite having wrought them with joints of love. . . .
> (DK 31B fr. 87)
> From both eyes one vision is produced. (DK 31B fr. 88)

This last fragment ends abruptly, but it shows that Empedocles saw a problem where others saw none: trait of a true research worker.

The repeated expression "untiring" indicates that Empedocles felt there was a difference between sensations, like smell and taste, whose emitting substances are sooner or later exhausted, and sight, whose source is in principle inexhaustible; hence that sight is not solely a matter of "effluvia" entering the eye.

We need to remember that the sudden conversion of stimuli into actual sensation can only be stated and not fully conceived even today, as has already been pointed out, although we know more about the correlations between sensation and the afferent nerves, as well as between certain parts of the brain.

About Empdocles' theory on the sensation of hearing, we have only a half-verse: "A bell . . . a fleshy outcrop." (DK 31B fr. 99) I prefer the rendering "outcrop," "appendage," to the usual translations by twig. Theophrastus seems to have accepted this view, for in his *De Sensu* he comments: "Hearing is produced by the noises inside (the ear); that is, when the air is moved by the voice, it sounds inside; as if hearing were a bell, moved by the corresponding sounds, which (bell) being moved, strikes the walls of the ear and makes a sound." (DOX, p. 506) Aristotle, summing up Empedocles' theory of sensation, says "to some it seems that each (creature) experiences sensation through some passages through which the cause of the sensation enters in its main and extreme form, and they say we see and hear and have all other sensations in this way; also that things are seen through air and water, and other transparent media by having passages, invisible because of their smallness, but thickly placed in rows, and the transparent substances have them more than others. Those giving these definitions, like Empedocles, maintain these things not only about the causes of the sensation and the subjects experiencing it, but add that there is a mixture of the two, when the passages are of corresponding proportions." (AGC, 8, 324b ff.) Theophrastus points out that Empedocles says nothing about the sense of touch, except to repeat the general theory that it occurs through the correspondence of the passages (in the skin) to the stimuli. Aristotle's criticism of the whole conception is wide of the mark; it would not be necessary, he says, for the stimuli to penetrate into the passages, it would be enough if they just touched their entrances. He adds that no difference is made between animate and inanimate things, although the latter also have "passages." This is related to his general misunderstanding, which has already been pointed out.

The weakness of Empedocles' theory of sensation, in my opinion, lies elsewhere: that he thinks the seat of feeling and thought is not in the brain, but in the blood. We have only one fragment referring to this question, but it is explicit:

> Nourished in the blood-stream leaping back and forth
> (the heart) there thought, as called by men, reigns.
> For the blood round the heart is thought for the mortals.
>
> (DK 31B fr. 105)

This is without doubt a retrograde step, as already a generation before him Alcmeon, the great Pythagorean doctor, had located the seat both of sensation and thought in the brain. Smell, according to Alcmeon, goes through the breathing straight to the brain; all other sensations are also, in one way or another, as Theophrastus says, connected with the brain. (DOX, p. 506) To explain this retrograde conception of Empedocles, we must refer to his belief that all living creatures are akin to each other—"All creatures breathe in and out, and all have a share in feeling and thought." If all animals have the power to think and if in many animals there is no detectable brain while blood is common to all, then blood must be the centre of both sensation and knowledge. Incidentally, this total ignoring of Alcmeon reinforces our view that Empedocles came into contact with the Pythagoreans late in life, perhaps in his fifties, when the great figures of the immediate successors of Pythagoras had already receded to dim memory and oral tradition; and after he himself had completed his work *On Nature*.

That *something* travels from the source of the sensation to the sense-organ and that that something is different for each sense, more material in the sense of smell and taste, less in hearing and sight, is in my opinion one of the chief merits of Empedocles' general view of sensation. As all things, animate and inanimate, are composed of the four elements, this means in the last resort that each element in the sense-organ *analyses* the impressions it receives into its component elements. (In fact, Empedocles presupposes an elaboration which we now know to take place in the center of the nerve-system, though on a different basis.) In Empedocles' view, we perceive the objects of the external world by the element that predominates in each of them and he refers to two distinct processes: (a) Each of the elements constituting a living being grows by the addition of its like: "Earth grows in bulk from earth, and ether from ether." (DK 31B, fr. 38) (b) The hypothesis that we recognize or conceive like by like.

> This is extended to feelings, like love and hatred:
> Likewise Love by Love we know, Hate by dire Hate.
>
> (DK 31B fr. 109)

Another fragment is rather enigmatic; for it extends the perception of growing of like by like to the qualities of hot and cold, humid and dry (a notion which later became traditional in Greek philosophy to its great disadvantage, for these qualities are not something existing by themselves, but are relative).

> Thus sweet seized upon sweet, and bitter sprang on bitter
> sour rushed for sour, and hot rode upon hot.
>
> (DK 31B fr. 90; W. E. Leonard's translation)

These verses (quoted by Plutarch—PQC, IV, 1, 3, 663A) seem of rather doubtful authenticity. First, because they are the only ones mentioning these qualities of bitter, sweet, and sour; second, because of the deliberate choice of a different verb for a similar process, contrary to Empedocles' custom.

Summing up, we can distinguish three chief concepts in Empedocles' theory of sensation:

(1) His primary idea: There are invisible emanations from all things, penetrating through equally invisible passages into the body of the recipient. These paths are of differing make and size, each sense-organ receiving the emanation appropriate to it; emanations destined to one sense-organ make no impression on another. In this respect all sensation is on an equal level, the smell sniffed by the hound, and the sight of a distant star. This is a definite progress on previous philosophers,

none of whom attempted to formulate a coherent theory of sensation: it is also consistent with modern science.

(2) His attempt at explanation: As we are made up of the same elements as everything in existence, when we recognize things by the senses, it must be because the like in us recognizes the like in them.

(3) His extension of this idea of like attracting and recognizing like from sensible qualities to the feelings.

The retrograde element in Empedocles' theory is that he makes the blood the seat not only of sensation but also of thought. This, as we said, was inexcusable, since the system of Alcmeon was already current in his time.

Knowledge. However the sensations may be produced, and whatever the central organ which receives the stimuli may be, the central question for a philosopher is: Do sensations give a true picture of the external world; are the images they occasion a trustworthy evidence as to the constitution of the world? Empedocles' answer to this question is a "double truth," as are all his answers, and it is difficult to reconcile all the fragments dealing with this subject, unless we distinguish the world as it presents itself to us—the visible, audible olfactory world with its endless variety—from its true constitution; that is, the elements and the forces.

On the first level, the senses convey reliable evidence, if we know how to delimit their bounds. The philosopher warns his disciple not to rely exclusively on one sense, and not to believe one more than the others:

> But come, consider with all thy mental power how each thing
> is revealed:
> trusting sight not more than hearing, and resounding noise
> not more than prowess of tongue; nor must thou hinder from
> they limbs
> any of the other means by which there is access to knowledg,
> but understand each thing in the way in which it is best revealed.
>
> (DK 31B fr. 3)

The word "understand" or "conceive" is, I think, the key word.

It stresses that intellectual elaboration is needed before we can trust the evidence of the senses. For if we were advised to accept that evidence in the verses preceding this part of the fragment (which contain a rigmarole about the white-armed virgin Muse in the well-reined chariot of song), the advice (in reality to himself) not to reveal more than is meet for ephemeral mortals to hear etc. would be meaningless. Sight and hearing and "prowess of tongue" (probably the discourse of other philosophers) are not to be rejected outright. They can convey some knowledge, if one knows how to sift their evidence. For this sifting, something more than the senses is needed—intellect or intuitions or Nous.

This is corroborated by a number of fragments; but before we give them, it is worth stressing once more that Empedocles does not reject outright the evidence of the senses. The wise man should not despise them as Parmenides and Heraclitus did and as Plato was to do later.

The great care devoted by Empedocles to tracing both the origin and the function of each sensation shows that he attached a certain value to them. How far does this value extend? It cannot show us the invisible passages, nor the effluvia emanating from the objects of perception, nor can it inform us of the real constituents of the perceptible world: the elements, their combination within each object, and the forces working to establish or to dissolve this composition. But though sensations cannot initiate us into the inner truth of the reality, they can indicate "how each thing is revealed." This means that they are the raw material of higher knowledge, a first step upon the ascending ladder of true knowledge.

No one has seen "Amity working her way" among the elements nor mixing the various elements, putting "a little less here, a little more there"; nor "leading the mute throng of abundantly spawning fish." Nor can sensation persuade us that birth and death are nothing but the coming together and the separation of the elements; hence that we should not rejoice over the one, nor grieve over the other. Sensation is often the cause of the ills and cares that blunt the wits of mortals; and unless we assign sensations to their proper place, they can give rise to errors so far as the deeper truth of things is concerned. But even the faulty impressions created by sensations can give an intimation of what is that true reality. Empedocles confesses that although he himself is aware of the insubstantiality of birth and death as realities, yet he talks like the rest of mankind "by force of usage."

> When having come together in the proper mixture,
> (the elements) rise to the light in the shape of a man,
> or as beasts living in the wild, or as bushes or birds,
> Then people call it birth and creation; and when they separate
> they call it ill-fated death. I, too, talk like that
> by force of usage. (DK, 31B fr. 9)

And he tells us that the wise man,

> . . . must join many peaks (of thought) one to the other,
> and not follow exclusively one path. (DK, 31B fr. 24)

One fragment indicates how knowledge can be imparted by hearing: "Listen thou to my words, for learning increases intellectual power"; and, later in the same fragment: "Listen to utterance of words that do not deceive." (DK, 31B fr. 14) But the exceptional man must go beyond the sensations. How can he do this? By thinking; by looking "with the mind." The speculative thinker "must join many peaks (of thought) one to the other, and not follow exclusively one path" of words. (DK, 31B fr. 24) This line sketches a method of intellectual work as Empedocles conceived it. One starts from the ground level, plodding up one peak and then the next. Later one may discover a short-cut to the summit and finally one may soar over all the peaks, joining them together by invisible paths.

If therefore sensations, and their combinations in memory by words and analytical thinking, are not sufficient to form ideas, opinions, and lastly knowledge (Alcmeon believed they were), what is the source of true knowledge, even assuming that only few men can rise to it? The traditional answer was intuition or revelation. Roughly speaking, we may say that Empedocles accepted the first in his work *On Nature*, and the second in his *Purifications*. Intuition, though it appears suddenly, is the result of a long period of preparation, of thinking or brooding over a problem, of a strenuous elaboration of phenomena empirically acquired. This appears to be the way chosen by Empedocles. It does not exclude the existence of a mind outside man—either divine or something like the "Xynos Nous" of Heraclitus—a mind permeating the universe, diffused throughout the world, from which the wise man can draw more than the common run of mankind. But Empedocles nowhere explicitly refers to such a source in *On Nature*, despite his appeals to the Muse, or to the gods, not to let him be misled by "tongues prattling to no purpose." The strongest instance of this kind of interpretation is:

> Ye gods, turn madness away from my tongue,
> and let through consecrated lips a clear spring flow;
> and I beseech thee, white-armed virgin Muse . . .
>
> (DK, 31B fr. 3)

There follow a number of trite and unpoetic allusions—part of the stock-in-trade of the imitators of Homer—which moreover suffer from mixed metaphors and end in nonsense. Such allusions appealed to the decadent ages which preserved them for us, at the expense of who knows how many deep and original thoughts. Yet the opening phrase is beautiful. Empedocles may not have believed in the traditional gods, but there are moments in which one wants to invoke or to beseech something outside oneself. Another fragment from the Purifications stresses the same need:

> If thou, immortal Muse, ever wast inclined
> to spend thy care in favor of one of the mortal men,
> be now with me, thy worshipper,
> when I intend to reveal virtuous words about the blessed gods.
>
> (DK, 31B fr. 131)

It is to be doubted whether this verbiage of mystification has anything to do with the vow of secrecy imposed on its members by the Pythagorean school. For this school believed knowledge to be not a gift from the gods but a revelation of the ultimate essence of the world, the key to which was held only by themselves.

I take these two fragments as a remote echo from the influence exercised by Parmenides in Empedocles' young days. The whole of the first fragment of Parmenides' work deals with a chariot which carried him to the borders of Day and Night, led by the virgin daughters of the Sun, and brought him to a great Gate where the Sun's daughters stripped away the veils etc. etc. In any interpretation of the philosophy of either of these thinkers, these fragments are irrelevant.

The passage quoted from Empedocles do not convince us that he believed in a higher-than-human source of knowledge. To revert therefore to the way in which a superior man can attain true knowledge, the philosopher sketches a much more sober method by which such knowledge may be reached, in another fragment. Moral qualities, as well as intellectual capacity and effort, are stressed as prerequisites: persistence, single-mindedness, and disinterestedness. But do not such qualities go hand in hand with genius? Here is the whole remarkable fragment:

> For if thou adherest to these things steadfastly in thy
>   strong mind,
> considering them with good intent and selfless pure study,
> they'll all be with thee throughout thy life in a high degree,
> and thou wilt have acquired much else from them,
> for they increase themselves in stature, each according to his
>   nature.
> But if thou longest for other things, such as are common to men,
> in thousands of base desires which blunt the intellectual might,
> why then they'll soon leave thee with time's passing,
> wishing to rejoin their own kindred race.
> For know that all beings have a share in wisdom and thought.
>   (DK, 31B fr. 110)

What is the "kindred race" to which high thoughts may wish to return? It must be other minds, better fitted to receive them, whether human or belonging to other creatures.

We have seen that, on the lower level, sensations carried to us from the external things (through the invisible passages scattered over the body) inform us of the objects of this world. We have also seen that this world is not to be despised; but that knowledge does not carry us very far. In the first place, it is contingent; men go by what "they happen to come across" and then boast to have perceived the whole, which is impossible. Secondly, that knowledge does not convey a true picture of the ultimate reality, nor of life and death, which are nothing but the coming together and the separation of the elements. Men have a dim understanding of the working not only of the cosmic process, but also of the influence of Amity in their affairs.

How the step takes place from the lower to the higher level of knowledge we are not told. Empedocles feels keenly that what he has to say about the higher level is inconceivable and almost impossible to express by the available linguistic means. He therefore returns again and again to the subject of the elements and the forces, and the word "deficient" recurs many times in his verses. As far as I know, he is the only philosopher (pre- or post-Socratic) to have acknowledged himself baffled by the gap between what he has conceived, and what it is possible to express adequately. This modesty, despite his assured statements, is a sign of a truly philosophical mind; for he could not be unaware that his repetitions and hesitations might make him the butt of adverse criticism. We have already quoted fragments that show this uncertainty, and another begins:

> If explanation of these things seems to thee somewhat deficient,
> and thou wonderest how, from earth and water and air,
> and the sun's fire, being mixed, so many mortal kinds of creatures
> of so many colors, as now enjoy life, fitted together by
> Aphrodite.   (DK, 31B fr. 71)

The fragment ends here.

Yet, despite the difficulty in expressing the higher level of knowledge by use of the common language, Empedocles insists that all other knowledge is contingent and superficial. People who merely trust their senses and their personal experience learn nothing of the truth:

> According to their circumstances grow the thoughts of men.
> (DK, 31 B fr. 103)

Hence their thoughts can have no general validity. Again:

> As they change and become different, so for them
> their thoughts present themselves and become different
> every time. (DK, 31B fr. 108)

It should be mentioned here that, though Aristotle interprets the verses as we do—that the changes of thought occur according to what happens to people or to the changes that take place in themselves (AA, III, iii, 427a; AMP. V, 1009b) later commentators (Philoponos and Simplicius) connect the second fragment to the change of disposition men suffer in their sleep. There is nothing in the fragment itself to suggest this interpretation, and if there had been anything in its original context, Aristotle could not have failed to mention it.

It seems therefore that, although Empedocles does not reject the evidence of the senses so far as the observable phenomena are concerned, the higher level of true knowledge comprises the composition of all things out of the four elements, the law governing their changes, the two forces reigning in turn over the world, and the cyclic cosmic process. There is no direct way from the one level to the other. They are different in quality. The lower level is contingent, the higher one is absolute. But various fragments inform us of the prerequisites for real and deep knowledge. The wise man must try to join the peaks of thought by many different ways. He must experiment in his mind, and, trying to form a consistent picture, reject much, retain little, and mould the pieces together with "pure intent." If faithfully adhered to and strenuously pursued, these will prepare the ground for a man to become receptive of the higher truth. We know already some of those conditions: single-mindedness, constant pondering over the same problem, steadfastness and detachment from any favorable or unfavorable appreciation by other people, whether these be the populace, or the so-called wise men.

These are moral attitudes. But there is also the unremitting intellectual effort, the *tensing* of the whole mental apparatus. Though "these things can neither be seen nor heard by men, nor concerned by the mind," (DK, 31B fr. 2), yet the advice is given again and again to understand by intellect: "understand how each thing is revealed." (DK, 31B fr. 3) The apparent contradiction of trying to understand things "not conceivable by intellect" may be tentatively solved by considering "intellect" as having two meanings: analytical or discursive thinking, and the deeper, intuitive conception—what the ancients meant by Logos. Experience also shows that intellectual effort increases understanding not only of specific problems, but of other things as well (as learning to play one piece well on one instrument makes one more capable of performing other pieces): "Knowledge makes the mind grow." (DK, 31b fr. 17) In short, Empedocles believes in the creativeness of the human, or more-than-ordinary-human mind, loosened from the bondage of ambition, from the multifarious demands of everyday life. Empedocles also trusts what we should nowadays call the subconscious working of the mind, when problems, seemingly insoluble to the discursive thought, are suddenly illuminated and fall into place of their own accord. All this is summarised in the stern advice he gives to his disciple Pausanias in:

> For if thou adherest to these things steadfastly in thy
>   strong mind,
> considering them with good intent and selfless pure study,
> they'll all be with thee throughout thy life in a high degree,
> and thou wilt have acquired much else from them.
> For they increase themselves in stature, each according to its
>   nature.
> But if thou longest for other things, such as are common to men
> in thousands of base desires, which blunt the intellectual might,
> Why then, they'll soon leave thee with time's passing,
> wishing to rejoin their kindred race.   (DK, 31B fr. 110)

This is perfect advice for all disinterested study, research, or pondering; valid today as much as in Empedocles' time. For moral disposition is not alien to intellectual pursuit, but supports it; and the process going on in our minds, even while we are not conscious of it, "increases itself" unless we are drawn away from our pure intent by "thousands of base desires." The outcome is not guaranteed by these prerequisites; but they are indispensable.

Awareness that this ceaseless intellectual effort is a thankless task from the point of view of earthly honors and happiness is expressed in a remarkable fragment of the *Purifications*.

> Oh, my friends, I know that truth is with the words I shall utter,
> but toilsome and heavy and a cause of envy to men
> is the onrush of knowledge into their minds.   (DK, 31B fr. 114)

This toil may be impaired by idle talk:

> ... shelter (these teachings) in thy silent breast.
>
> > (DK, 31B fr. 5)

But knowledge is not passive or static; it is a movement within one's breast; and one cannot know exactly when this movement will occur. Hence, after warning his disciple about the common man's aversion to superior minds, Empedocles advises:

> Do thou recognise the pledge of our Muse, and the orders
> she gives, once the spirit hath moved within thy breast.
>
> > (DK, 31B fr. 4)

Recapitulation. For Empedocles, there are many ways to higher knowledge. None of them guarantees that it will be reached: One must feel not merely that the effort is worthwhile, but that one cannot live without making it. The first and easiest beginning is through the senses on their own level; but their evidence must be sifted and recognized for what it is. There is no reason to trust one sense-organ more than another; each has a specific function and they must not be confused. There is nothing in Empedocles of Parmenides' outright rejection of all sense perception as a deception nor of Plato's advice to the would-be philosopher to study "dying and being dead." However the senses can give no knowledge of the real truth: of the laws of the elements, the forces, and the cosmic cycle, which are valid not only for human beings, but for the heavens and the gods themselves—imposing on them dissolution and a periodic return to the Sphairos. Higher knowledge may be reached only by the qualities described: unremitting concentration and "pure intent." Empedocles does not tell us explicitly how he came to his general conception of the laws of the universe, which constitute the kernel of his system. But he is absolutely certain of the truth of his doctrine: his words do not deceive, his Muse (in this context his inspiration) guarantees the truthfulness of his utterance. In addition to the fragment referring to Pythagoras, (DK, 31B fr. 129), he claims for himself alone the absolute superior and certain knowledge of the law of the universe:

> There is no man so wise that he could guess in his mind;
> that while they live—what they call life—
> there happen to them things good and bad. But before (the
>   elements)
> adhered together, and after they have separated, they were,
> and are, nothing at all.   (DK, 31B fr. 15)

The ultimate conception by Empedocles of the universal law of becoming, of the composition of everything, animate and inanimate out of the same ingredients, and of the recurrence of world upon world, identical or a little different as the proportions of the element's mixture varies (" a little more here, or a little less in relation to the other quantities" DK, 31B fr. 98) is not far removed from the conception that atoms differ only in the number and arrangement of their electrons, whose revolutions become immensely complicated as the number increases. On the level of immediate sense data, Empedocles not only kept in touch with the visible world, but carried out direct experiments, some of which achieved beneficial results; such as checking epidemics by stopping a pestilential wind and diverting a river course. These and other experiments may have led him to incorrect conclusions, but they all went to prove something.

One of his less well-known experiments was the following: Heraclitus, playing as usual with opposite notions, had said that sea water is poison to man, but nourishment to fish. Empedocles conceived the fantastic idea that there is sweet water in the sea. He was followed in this by Democritus, Aristotle, and Theophrastus, according to Aelian (*De Natura Animalium* IX, 64). To prove his idea, Empedocles lowered into the sea an empty vessel, sealed and made of wax. When he drew it up after twenty-four hours, the vessel was filled with sweet, drinkable water. Aristotle seems to have appropriated the experiment, adding only that Empedocles shared his view. Empedocles' conclusion in this case was not precise; but how many men adrift on the sea might have been saved from a horrible death by thirst if they had provided themselves with vessels of wax? Thus does man stumble on one truth while seeking for another.

Whether such experiments helped Empedocles to arrive at his conception of the elements and their laws, we do not know. But he was conscious that knowledge acquired on this level—power over nature—led to power over man. This is expressed, though vaguely, in the last fragment of *On Nature*, where he promises his disciple power and achievements, some of which have now been attained, while others still remain in the region of dreams.

> And all the medicines that are, to keep away old age and sickness,
> thou wilt learn, for only to thee shall I these things reveal.
> Thou wilt stop the violence of tireless winds, which, rising
> out of the earth, destroy by their breath meadows and fields;
> and again, at thy will, new-risen winds will rush.
> From darkling rain wilt thou cause dry weather, appropriate to
>   men's needs,
> and in the drought of summer wilt thou call forth
> tree-nourishing streams and the branches will reach up to heaven.
> From the Netherworld thou wilt bring back the vital force of a
>   man already dead.   (DK, 31B fr. 111)

6. BIOLOGY

The imaginative insights of Empedocles into the laws of biology are among the most interesting parts of his teaching: on the one hand, his detailed examination of the visible world and, on the other, his relation of what has happened in the stages of the cosmic cycle to the present.

Parallel with and in contrast to Empedocles' two main theories of comparative morphology and of evolution, we have many detailed fragments telling us of the composition of various parts and organs of living bodies. These will be discussed first, as they show Empedocles must have carried out some rudimentary anatomical experiments, that his curiosity about the phenomena of life on this earth was insatiable, and his interest unflagging. They also make clear that always at the base of all his observations and experiments there was his preconceived idea of the proportions of the four basic elements contained in each body and in its parts. For example, he tells us that our bones are made up of definite proportions of the elements of earth: one part of earth, four of fire, two of water, and one of air. But the elements in their pure form were undetectable, and there was no way of analyzing a bone into its constituent elements. Hence the proportions mentioned were pure guesses, and we are not told how those guesses were arrived at. Often, from a more or less correct factual observation, Empedocles drew wrong conclusions. Guesses are not excluded in science; but they take the form of provisional hypotheses, to be proved true or false by subsequent experiments.

Some of Empedocles' guesses, however, have since been proven fundamentally right, anticipating scientific discovery by more than two thousand years. These include the circulation of the blood, respiration through the pores of the skin, and the homologue between similar organs in different animal species. The system of breathing is described in detail in one of the longer and most beautiful fragments, where he compares the process to a clepsydra—a water-clock—with which a young girl is playing, sometimes stopping the tubes with her tender fingers (in which case the water cannot flow out), then letting it free. "All creatures breathe in and out in this way" says Empedocles, once more emphasizing the kinship between all living beings. In Empedocles' view, the body was perforated by invisible "bloodless" passages, through which the air could circulate; but blood could not rush out of them, because it is thicker than air. As the fingers of the girl stop up the tube of the water clock, the "resplendent water" cannot rush out, because it is held back by the air within the tube. Then the finger is withdrawn, the air rushes in from outside and pushes the water/blood down; and so it goes on alternatively. It is worth giving the whole fragment, bearing in mind that water here plays the role of the blood:

> Thus do all creatures breathe in and out; in all of them tubes
> of bloodless flesh are ranged along the surface of the body
> with tiny holes at their endings, so that they hold in
> the blood, but leave a free passage to the air.
> From these later, when the tender blood has retreated,
> the air rushes in swirling in storm-like waves; then, however,
> the air is again pushed out, and its withdrawal makes creatures
>   breath out.
> As when a young girl, playing with a clepsydra of gleaming
>   bronze,
> puts her tender finger in the opening, and dips it
> in the silvery water, no water can penetrate at the other end;
> for the air's weight hinders it from inside, at the fine ends
> of the perforated passage, closely placed together. But later,
> the air being exhausted, when the girl frees the opening and
>   lets out
> the thickened stream of the air, there is then a gap through which

there enters a corresponding mass of water.
In the same way, when the water occupies the depths of the
    vessel,
when the entrance and the passage is again stopped by the
    human hand,
the air from outside, imprisoned in the vessel,
prevents the water from rushing out, putting its strength
against the gates of the resounding bronze
until the hand is taken away. Then, in the opposite direction,
the air rushes in and the corresponding mass of water
runs under and emerges. In the same way, the tender blood
branching throughout the limbs, when it retreats backwards
to the inner depths (of the body) the stream of air rushes in again
in swelling waves, which, when it swells back, it breathes out
    an equal part of the air.   (DK, 31B fr. 100)

This fragment, though beautiful and poetic, justifies to a certain
extent Aristotle's contention that Empedocles repeats himself very
often; for it describes the process twice over, and because of the
metaphorical expressions he uses, it is not always clear where the
first round, so to say, ends and the second begins. But the meaning
is clear: air cannot enter as long as the blood is near the surface,
though the blood cannot run out of the tiny passages, which hem
it in while they let the air through. Thus as the blood rushes
towards the surface of the body, air is pushed out and we have
breathing out. When the blood retreats to the inside of the body,
the air can rush in and perform whatever function it has to (oxy-
genating the blood as we would say today). We have already seen,
in Empedocles' simile of the lantern, that the thinness of the fire
can pass through its thin horn sides, although the air is too thick to
penetrate inside. In the case of the water clock, the air plays the
role of the fire of the lantern, and the blood there plays the role
of the air.

Other details of the biological theories of Empedocles are those
concerning conception and pregnancy, as well as the formation of
the embryo. He believes, probably through an autopsy on women
who died during pregnancy, that the embryo takes a distinct human form after the 49th day, which is not very far from the ascertained facts. Because of his preconceived idea of the supremacy of

the male, he believed, erroneously, that male children are nurtured on the "warmer" right-hand side of the womb and females on the left and cooler side. But he had astonishing insights into the procreation of abnormal births, which, he says, are produced because of the excess or deficiency of the sperm, irregular movements during the moment of conception, the division of the sperm in too many parts, or because of lack of breathing (presumably at the moment of birth): "thus summing up all the possible causes," says Aetius. (DOX, pp. 420,421) Twins are born because of the ascission of one fertilized egg. Aetius reports a detailed description of how the first breath was taken by the first animal born, which would apply equally to each new-born baby: "The dampness inside the embryo recedes because of the dryness of the outer air and so the air rushes in to fill the emptiness thus created." (DOX, p. 411) And Soranus (cf. his *Gynaecology*) knows about Empedocles having located the four blood vessels, two arteries and two veins, converging in the womb and feeding the embryo, adding that, according to Empedocles, they issue out of the liver. Side by side with some unfounded views, such as that some pregnancies last longer because the prehistoric day at first lasted ten months and was later reduced to eight, we have flashes of insight that anticipate discoveries of our own century: children grow to resemble one or other of their parents because of the *dominance* of the qualities in the sperm or the egg of that parent. (DOX, p. 422) By Empedocles this is attributed, says Aetius (DOX, p. 422), to one of two causes, physical or mental: either to the humidity of the semen having evaporated, or to the imagination of the woman at the moment of conception; for it is well-known, he adds, that women have fallen in love with statues of gods or heroes, and have then given birth to children resembling them. (cf. Hippocrates, *De Genit.* 8, vii)

There are many other reports of points connected with Empedocles' views on pregnancy and conception of which, however, there is no hint in the existing fragments. The above is enough to show the detailed preoccupation of the philosopher with concrete and ascertainable facts, and his insights into the mechanism of these fundamental functions. He seems also to have applied himself to matters concerning the procreation of animals. A question which exercised the minds of the ancient philosophers and of later commentators was, why mules are sterile. Empedocles is said to have applied the same general rules which inform his biology as a whole and explained it as either because of the narrowness of the passage to the womb, or because of the excessive thickness or thinness of the semen. However, we have no fragment concerning this matter but only second-hand reports.

On plants Empedocles seems to have had as definite views as on animals and men, though the relevant fragments are few and short. He maintained that the plants draw their nourishment from two sources—the roots from the earth, and the leaves from the air. Theophrastus, influenced as always by Aristotle, thinks this absurd; but Empedocles' conception has been grandly vindicated by modern science. He has pithy characteristic adjectives for many kinds of trees that show acute observation: he talks about "late-ripening pomegranates" and "apples with thick skin." This last caused great controversy among ancient commentators. Plutarch admits he was puzzled by the word I have rendered by "thick skin." (PQC, V, 8, 2, 683 D/E) He asked some grammarians about it, and found "that it was applied to the apples because of their abundant ripening, for abundance and juicy ripening is called so by the poets. . . . A cognate word was also applied to Dionysus, they said." The long duration of the apples' prime and their plentiful juice seems therefore to have inspired Empedocles to call them that. But the orginal meaning of the word "phloios" is skin or rind. The apple is not a particularly juicy fruit, even today, after so much crossing and care has been bestowed on it, and wild apples are dry and astringent. Moreover, the use of the word "phloios" appears in the very next fragment, undoubtedly in the meaning I have given it.

Empedocles seems to have maintained (no fragment is extant) that trees emerged before the animals and even before the sun started on its course. They were nourished by the heat of the interior of the earth, so that they were parts of the earth in the same way as embryos are part of the mother's body. (DOX, p. 438) Aetius goes on to explain that Empedocles attributed the difference between deciduous and evergreen plants to the difference of moisture inside the parts of the tree. This is not worse than the example Aristotle gives in one of his syllogisms, that plants with wide leaves shed them in winter, which he could have easily ascertained was false.

Ancient criticism of Empedocles' biological views was generally adverse. Aristotle begins with his usual "Empedocles is not right in saying . . .," insisting that there must be one cause of birth and growth and not two, whereas Empedocles stated that growth was due to the action of warmth on the roots, and of fire (presumably the sun) on the leaves. It is amazing how often ancient comment is adverse to precisely the parts of Empedocles' doctrine that have been vindicated by modern science. In general Aristotle's criticism is bedeviled by his own distinction between matter or nature and form or spirit, which was not part of Empedocles' theory. Empedocles, as we have seen, thought nothing about personal immortality, believing the soul to be a harmonious relation between all the functions of the body, an opinion voiced in Plato's *Phaedo* by one of the Theban Pythagoreans present on the last day before Socrates' death. Aristotle therefore finds contradictions that do not exist. To cite one of many examples: Aristotle criticized Empedocles' repeated assertions that "before the elements came up to the light of day in the form of a lion or a man" (that is, before they coalesced to form this creature) and after the elements composing them were dispersed, the creatures were nothing at all. "But," says Aristotle "nature is the principle rather than matter." (APA, I, 1, 642a) In *de Anima* (I, iv, 408a) Aristotle continues the same argument, but in an obverse manner. He attacks the "proportion" for the soul. The mixture cannot be in the same proportion as in flesh and bone for then there would be many souls scattered all over the body: "One would like to ask Empedocles the following: which of the two is a fact? Is the proportion the soul? Or rather does the soul, being something else, come into the limbs?" And again: "Is Love the cause of all the fortuitous mixtures, or only of the one existing in accordance to the law?" "And is the soul the law, or is it something else in addition to the law?" In his *Metaphysica* (XII, x, 1075) Aristotle takes up the same ques-

tion again, posing the same dilemmas, which are in fact quite un-
related to Empedocles' theory.

Other parts of Aristotle's criticism are more justified, for example, as against the idea that the most warm-blooded animals live
in the sea to escape from the excess of heat in their nature. (ADR,
XIV, 477b) Theophrastus follows Aristotle's criticism in about the
same words.

There are some general laws in Empedocles' biology which concern classes and not species of animals, plants and phenomena, inspired partly by his medical knowledge, and partly by his intuitive and imaginative conception of the kinship of all living creatures: he had observed, for instance, that there is fermentation if
you leave water inside a container made from tree-bark, and he
compares digestion to fermentation. This is not contained in any
of the fragments but is attested by Galen, who says that the Hip-
pocrateans call digestion what Empedocles calls fermentation.

We should note that, in the fragment on respiration quoted
earlier, Empedocles speaks of "all creatures" breathing in and out.
In his belief that everything living has a share in feeling and
thought, he differed from the Pythagorean doctor Alcmeon, who
attributed feelings to animals but not thought.

The more one reads and ponders over Empedocles' few and
scattered fragments on biological questions, the more one wonders
at his perspicacity, which thought no phenomenon unworthy of
attention; and the more one regrets that so little of his biological
writings have been preserved. He made many wrong guesses, but
his discovery of the circulation of the blood and of the invisible
respiration through the skin are sufficient to establish his claim to
be a forerunner of modern science in biology.

Comparative Morphology. But there is more than that: Empedocles realized that all living creatures have features that perform analogous functions, though their contingent variety may
give these features, or organs, different shapes and textures resulting from the contingent formation of the various species. Hence
we have to distinguish between an apparent dissimilarity of form,
and a basic resemblance in the functions they perform: feeding,

protecting, procreating. This is the first appearance in history of comparative morphology as a coherent and general notion, under which the most varied phenomena may be subsumed. The decisive fragment is:

> Hair and skin and the foliage of trees, and the thick plumage
> of birds, and the scales of fish, are the same on their sturdy limbs.
> (DK, 31B fr. 82)

"The same" means that they serve the same purpose: to protect the body from the weather or from the medium in which each species lives, or to protect the seed from enemy attacks. The foliage protects the fruit, and hence the seed, from wind and rain as the thick skin or pelt protects the terrestrial animals. The human race has learned to cover its body with alien skins or woven materials, hence its protective covering of hair has decayed, remaining only over its most vulnerable parts: the skull and the eyes (to shield them from sweat and flying particles of dust etc.) and the sexual organs, whose "shaggy" character Empedocles so frequently stresses. The following fragment should be interpreted in the same way, despite Plutarch's objection.

> . . . likewise on the hedgehog's back
> manes grow with sharp-pointed bristles.　　(DK, 31B fr. 82)

Plutarch assumes the hedgehog's bristles to correspond to weapons of attack: teeth, claws, stings. (PF, 3, 98D) But Empedocles meant to compare the bristles to hair, as is shown by the word "manes" and "back." One of Aristotle's objections was based on Empedocles' statement that bones were constituted of so much water, so much fire, etc; implying that all bones were constituted in the same way, "those of the lion, of the ox, and of man." Aristotle considers this an irrefutable reductio ad absurdum; but modern biology sides with Empedocles, especially as regards the bones of the higher mammals named by Aristotle.

Another stupendous analogy in comparative morphology is contained in the following few words:

Thus the tall trees, and first among them the olive-tree,
give birth to their eggs . . .   (DK, 31B fr. 79)

The analogy is marvelous and thorough. In the eggs of birds as in
fruit, the semen is in the middle (in the kernel or the yolk), surrounded by nourishing stuff.

Evolution. Omitting many more interesting details about various
biological phenomena, we come to the picture Empedocles formed
in his mind about the origin of living creatures, within each cycle
of the cosmic process. We have already seen the horrid representations of monsters, which were created by the havoc wrought by
Strife, after it first disturbed the uneffable harmony and unity of
the Sphairos. Then, in Empedocles' view, as the mild-mannered
onrush of Aphrodite penetrated into the middle of the vortex and
started to form harmonious combinations, all those monsters, unable to feed themselves or to procreate, died one by one. This
happened gradually, for not "blamelessly" did Aphrodite gain the
upper hand. The process was long and painful, and only gradually
were there produced the various forms we have seen, differing so
greatly in color and shape, "a wonder to behold."

Empedocles' conception of the original forms of the human
species was no doubt influenced by current mythological ideas:
out of the earth the cosmic fire, rushing to meet its own kin—the
fire in the ether or sky—threw up crude lumps of earthly creatures,
who had no distinct limbs, nor speech, nor genitals. They were
chancy creations, having practically no likeness to human form.
Then fire separated the two sexes, of "men and the much-be-
moaned (or deserving of tears) women, and their nature was clearly separated. (DK, 31B fr. 62) Memory (it is not clear whether
it is the memory of the time when both sexes were united, as in
Plato's *Symposium*) aided by sight made them desire each other.
(DK, 31B fr. 64) But there is also another version of a desirable
creation by Amity, who moulded the forms in clay, then dipped
or sprinkled them in water, and gave them to quick fire to make
them resistant. (DK, 31B fr. 73) This version is obviously model-
led on Prometheus, who also fashioned men out of clay, but gave

them fire to use consciously much later. It also reminds us of
Thetis holding Achilles over the fire to make him invulnerable
and of Demeter doing the same to Triptolemos.

Equally in the basic picture of original monsters combining in
unnatural and unharmonious shapes and surviving only if they
were able to feed themselves or to procreate, and in the contrasting picture of origin through Amity, chance plays a decisive role.
The expressions "as they happen to meet" and "by the will of
chance," and others like them, occur again and again. For example,
it is explained that some of the animals have the soft parts of their
body outside, while others are hard outside and soft inside, "having chanced to be moulded in this way in the palms of Amity."
(DK, 31B fr. 95)

Modern commentators have seen parts of the biological theory
of Empedocles as a primitive anticipation of Darwin's theory of
evolution. For Empedocles, as for Darwin, life is contingent.
Nature is a spendthrift, creating many unfit creatures, until some
succeed in surviving in sufficient numbers and procreating descendants also adapted to their surroundings. The contingency is ac-
counted for by Empedocles through the ever-continuing contest
between Strife and Amity, for Amity is not entirely free to fashion
the creatures she wants, but has to work with the materials—the
elements and their combinations—which she *happens* each time to
have at her disposal. She plays the role of the final cause, but only
so far as fortuitous circumstances allow.

This contingency, this role of chance, suggests—though Empedocles does not say so explicitly—that the return of the cosmic
cycle need not be absolutely identical each time. As Empedocles
is more a biologist than a physicist, he stresses repeatedly the "here
a little more, there a little less," and his determination as to the general lines of the cosmic cycle is tempered by an awareness of the
great variety of living creatures and plants that he observes. The
Pythagoreans, however—at least those of the second and third
generation—influenced by the unchanging qualities of numbers,
believed in the self-same repetition of every single event in every
cosmic cycle.

The forms pouring out when Strife withdraws are of myriads

of varieties, according to all sorts of models. They are also contingent. One could imagine another multitude, equally well fitted to their environment, which could also be "a wonder to behold." "Earth came together by chance with the other three (with fire and water and the resplendent ether), either a little less or a little more in relation to the other quantities. From these grew the blood and all the other kinds of flesh." (DK, 31B fr. 98) This fragment is of capital importance. Even air as an element "sometimes so upon its course happened to run, at other times otherwise." (DK, 31B fr. 53)

Life is contingent in its forms. However, in the cosmic process, life is bound to come after the Sphairos is broken up by Strife, when Amity painfully drives him back and begins moulding in her loving palms the various species. From the elements that "happened to come together," there will always be an ordered organic world. But many fragments indicate that the evolution in each of the cosmic cycles is not bound to the identical forms of the previous ones:

> These (the elements) are forever themselves, but running
> through each other they become at times different, yet
> are forever and ever the same.

and:

> For they (the elements) are always themselves, but
> running through each other, they take on various forms and
> shapes, so much does the mixture change them.

and:

> In so far as these never end changing throughout, in so far
> they are immovable in a circle.   (DK, 31B fr. 17, 21, 26)

Summing up. Summing up Empedocles' theories of evolution and of comparative morphology, we must stress four points:

(a) His view of the unity of all living organisms, extended even to the plants. Each in its own way grows the appropriate organs to protect itself against the outer world and the other living organisms. Therefore hair, skin, scales, etc. "are the same": they perform the same function. Each form of life is able to reproduce itself. "Desiring its kindred by the force of love," "the abundant spawn of fish, the fruit of the trees" are "the same." Love, Harmony, or Amity, one of the two cosmic forces (and the only divine power Empedocles worships) shapes everything in her "loving palms:" our eyes and bones and the tall trees, and the scaly monsters of the deep. It follows that all creatures have organs and functions that have much in common. All "breathe in and out;" all "rejoice and grieve" when the elements that compose them adhere together or fall apart; all are equally ephemeral. They were nothing at all before the elements that form them coalesced and they will be nothing once these have separated.

(b) In *On Nature* there is no scale of values. All the creatures together make the world "a wonder to behold:" the voiceless fish, the hedgehog, the tall trees, the lions, and the race of men and tearful women as well as the long-lived but not eternal gods. At the appropriate time, they will all be gathered together in the Sphairos, and become one whole; without qualities; without separate beings; without consciousness, joy, or grief; without earth, sun, sea, or "the immeasurable heights of the air"; without gods. But while the visible world lasts, the bush and the fish and the lions are as much the object of the care of Kypris as the race of men.

(c) To the question of whether the whole cycle comes round again and again owing to purely mechanistic laws, and is every time identical, it is difficult to give an answer. Certainly the cosmic cycle is decreed by fate. The Sphairos will at some time be broken up. Great Strife, rising to honors, will penetrate to the center and set the whole process going: "The limbs of the god (the Sphairos) shook all over, one after the other." Since the Sphairos itself has no limbs (no manly head, no swift moving knees, no two branching arms, etc), either the above is a poetic image or it means that the Sphairos has already ceased being itself; the elements are already flying apart, whirling about, meeting and separating as the movement carries them along.

(d) The part played by chance is clearly set forth. Even feeling and thinking are produced in living beings "by the will of chance," by "what they happen to come across." Only gradually will Aphrodite penetrate to the center, driving Strife to the outer edges of the cosmos, and mould in her palms harmonious creatures, able to survive and to reproduce themselves. However, she is not all-powerful, she has to work with what happens to be at hand and to make the best of contingencies—the lucky meeting of such-and-such at such-and-such a time, in such-and-such proportions. This suggests that the last details of the cosmic cycle are not predetermined and that the sway of Harmony may be at times more, and at other times a little less. Design is therefore superimposed on blind chance and is more or less successful. But contingency or chance is compelling. The repetition of expressions such as they "met by chance," "by the will of chance," etc.; the great variety of the forms of life each devouring the other; the profusion of procreation, only part of which will survive; the flying apart of the elements, which stupid people call "baneful death;" all these incline us to believe that only the great lines of the cosmic cycle are predetermined. The actual results are fortuitous, and different forms might result in the future, and perhaps have existed in the past. This contingency of the details leaves a crack open in the iron walls of the inescapable circle for a better arrangement, for a solution, like a salvation. The hint is too dim to build upon and Empedocles does not seem to have seriously envisaged it, for Love and Strife:

> As the two were of old, so they'll always be, nor ever, I think,
> will immeasurable time be emptied of them both.
>   (DK, 31B fr. 16)

Is it too fanciful to detect a note of hesitancy in the words "I think?" Yet the power of man can be increased a hundredfold, as the lines on Pythagoras suggests, and as Empedocles promised to his disciple Pausanias, who (Empedocles says) may win mastery over nature; hinder the winds or call them forth according to human interest; produce rain out of drought and vice-versa; find medicines against all ills and against old age; and "from the Netherworld bring back the vital force of a man already dead." (DK, 31B fr. 111) This last statement certainly contradicts the assertion that death and birth are mere names given by witless men to the coalescence and dispersion of the elements. For if man can prevent their dissolution by averting old age, and can reassemble them after they have dispersed, man must have penetrated to the inner secrets of nature and grasped the *pattern* according to which the elements can combine to produce live beings. The perspectives this opens are limitless.

More than a century ago, Auguste Comte defined the purpose of modern science as to "understand nature in order to master it." This is the same as the view expressed by Empedocles. In this, as well as in his first sketch of a theory of evolution and in his insights into comparative morphology, Empedocles is far more modern than is usually acknowledged.

7. COSMOLOGY

We refer to Empedocles' "cosmology" rather than his "cosmogony" because he did not believe in an absolute and unique creation of the universe but in a constant repetition of the emergence of the world after the periodically recurring peace of the Sphairos in which everything is merged together.

This part of his theory is the weakest, and it cannot be a coincidence that it is the part on which we have the fewest fragments. These are also very discontinued and brief. Indeed, there is hardly a fragment of more than two lines that deals with any part of his cosmology—on either astronomy or his general notions of the heavenly bodies etc.

Aristotle takes a hostile view towards all those "who make the heavens come into existence; Anaxagoras only once, Empedocles many times." (AC, 279b, 17; 301a) This repetition however isn't apparent in those scraps of sentences that the ancient commentators have transmitted to us. On the other hand, several other philosophers had also tried to describe the creation, some influenced by older legends embodied in the religious traditions of the Greeks (especially by Hesiod's *Theogony*), others influenced by imported cults, such as the Orphic and Dionysiac mysteries, as well as the Assyrian and Babylonian epics and the occult oral narrations of generations of Chaldean and Egyptian priests. For example, Xenophanes and Pherekydes stipulated many coexistent universes without any connection between them.

In building up his cosmology, Empedocles no doubt experienced the same influences. We have already mentioned that the "long year" of the Babylonians probably contributed to the formation of his idea of an eternal recurrence; it has been calculated that each year on earth corresponds to two minutes of that long year, which makes the Babylonian "long year" correspond to 262,800 earthly years; but if, as other scholars maintain, each earthly year corresponds to two *seconds* of the "long year," this number must be multiplied by sixty.

In addition to their shortness and lack of connection, the extant fragments referring to Empedocles' cosmology are beset by his unfortunate tendency to clothe his views in allegorical or poetic expressions that add little to our knowledge and at times make for confusion: "the sharp-arrowed sun and the mild-shining moon" (DK, 31B fr. 40) conveys little when preceded by nothing and followed by nothing.

We have therefore to turn to second-and third-hand evidence to form a picture of what Empedocles believed to be the repeated process of the world's creation, after the disturbance of the Sphairos. However, this evidence proves highly unreliable when it is compared with Empedocles' own few remaining fragments. The explanations given by the early commentators must often be rejected.

We know from Empedocles' extensive fragments on the cyclic process that in the Sphairos there was no sun or moon or stars. However, his cosmology does not go back as far as this and we can reconstruct from various reports that Empedocles believed the earth to lie in the middle of the visible universe, held in equilibrium by the swift rotation of two hemispheres; one light and one dark: the light one being a hemisphere of fire, which contains the sun. Eustathios (who admits he got his information from Clemens, who asserts he had it from Theophrastus) gives a long and confused account of the original creation, as expounded by Empedocles:

> . . . at first air was created all round. Then the fire ran out in a circle and the air, having nowhere else to go and compressed by the fire, became frozen. Then, whirled round by the fire, two hemispheres were created; the one consisting wholly of fire, the

other of air mixed with a little fire. The latter is, in Empedocles'
opinion, the dark hemisphere. The beginning of the movement
was caused by the collection (of elements) being disturbed and
rarefied by the onrush of fire. The sun that we see, he goes on,
is not by its nature a mass of fire, but is a reflection of that fire,
similar to the reflection thrown back by a surface of water. Empedocles says that the moon was constituted of old as an independent body by the air escaping from the fire, which was frozen
like hail; and that she has her light from the sun.

(DOX, 1, 18.10, 562)

The most coherent though very short report on Empedocles' cosmology is given by Diogenes Laertius: "He [Empedocles] says,
that the sun is a great mass of fire, and that it is larger than the
moon. The moon, on the other hand, has the shape of a lens; and
the sky is a fixed crystal dome." (DL, VIII, 77) Thus, according to
this report, it is not the sky that rotates, and the hemispheres must
be located outside of it. In the crystal dome of the sky there are
holes through which the fire of the outer space shines. These holes
are the fixed stars, while the planets (which, we must remember
included the sun and the moon) roam freely under the dome.

The Moon. To return to the shape of the moon and its relation
to the earth: Plutarch (probably the source of Diogenes Laertius'
story) states: "The shape of the moon, which changes twice in a
month, is described by Empedocles not as spherical, but rather as
a disc or a lens." (PQR, 101, 288B) He adds that Empedocles believes the moon to be a rock of frozen air, of the consistency of
hail, surrounded by fire. (POL, 5, 922C) Aëtius also mentions "the
moon's disclike shape" (DOX, 258) adding that it was Thales the
Milesian who first said that the moon is lighted by the sun. Many
other sources attribute this statement to Thales, and it is not improbable that the report is true, in view of the fact that Thales
accurately predicted several eclipses of the moon, and one of the
sun (which is considered by the astronomers much more difficult).
In a very beautiful single line of verse Empedocles tells us:

In a round orbit revolves round the earth the alien light.

(DK, 31B fr. 45)

The same thing, though stated more vaguely, must be meant by:

> Thus the light (of the sun) struck the wide circle of the moon.
>   (DK, 31B fr. 45)

Aëtius asserts that not only Thales held that the moon takes her light from the sun, but Pythagoras and Parmenides as well as Empedocles "taught likewise." (DOX, 350)
One fragment relating to the moon runs thus:

> [the moon] covers and hides its [the sun's] brilliance
> when it goes over it and plunges into darkness so much
> of the earth as the width of the blue-eyed crescent extends.
>   (DK, 31B fr. 42)

This takes care of the partial eclipses of the sun caused by the moon. Anaxagoras, who, according to Aristotle, was a few years older than Empedocles, but who began publishing his works later, knew that eclipses are caused by the earth's shadow intervening between the sun and the moon. Anaxagoras exerted considerable influence upon Pericles, and Plutarch, in his life of Pericles, mentions the following story, which shows how greatly Anaxagoras had freed his eminent pupil from current superstitions that eclipses were harbingers of calamity, or warnings from the gods. When an expedition led by Pericles was about to sail, there occurred an eclipse of the sun. The sailors, terrified, clamored for a postponement of the expedition. Pericles however simply covered his face for a few moments with his mantle and then uncovered it. "Has anything terrible happened?" he asked. And the expedition proceeded as planned. (PP, xxxv) Yet the superstition lived on, and a total eclipse of the moon in 413 B.C. was a major factor in the Athenian catastrophe in Sicily.

Another fragment has given rise to a lot of conjecture:

> She [the moon] looks straight onto the sacred face of her lord,
> standing opposite him.   (DK, 31B fr. 47)

I shall make so bold as to suggest a very naive interpretation: this probably refers to the wonderful sight when the full moon rises just as the sun is sinking and stands diametrically to him in the vault of heaven. Many such fragments, detached from their context, leave us with a fine picture in our minds, but without any understanding of the deeper significance of the phenomenon.

But Empedocles' most astonishing statement about the moon, for which we have no relevant fragment, is quoted by Plutarch. He first states: "But Aëtius says that Empedocles believes the moon is twice as far from the sun as she is from the earth," and then adds the following description of Empedocles' view (which must have originated from a genuine fragment, as Plutarch is incapable of such pithy ways of putting things): "The moon is very far from the sky (meaning the crystal dome) but is so near the earth that it almost touches it and revolves in its immediate neighbourhood; it somehow seems to graze its (the earth's) skin and revolve in the earth's embrace." (POL, 9, 925B) This makes the moon as nearly a satellite as the ancients had conceived this notion—the "embrace" being the earth's attraction—and shows once more the grandeur of Empedocles, who, by sheer intuitive guessing, anticipated scientific research by twenty centuries. Despite a number of objections on several points, Plutarch concludes that "nothing is left but to accept Empedocles' view that the light does not fall from one bright star (the sun) onto another (the moon), but that the moon is lighted by a reflection falling through darkness and night, and reaching us more weakly, as the "echo of a voice is weaker than the voice itself." (DOX, 350; POL, 16, 929E)

That is about all we can gather about the moon in Empedocles' cosmology. It is too little, but still enough to show his insatiable curiosity and the way he reached a number of correct conclusions from the very imperfect sense data, which were the only means of research he had at his disposal.

The Sun. We have already mentioned Eustathios' confused statement of Empedocles' idea of two suns: a fiery one travelling in the invisible hemisphere, and the one that we see, which is a reflection of the first. It should be stressed that the only extant fragment which remotely touches on this view states:

> [the sun] throws back its light towards Olympus with a fearless
>   face.   (DK, 31B fr. 44)

From his single word "back" it is difficult to build up these theories about a double sun and an invisible hemisphere. Also this fragment includes Empedocles' unfortunate habit of using ambiguous, mythological terms. In what sense is Olympus used here? It might mean the mountain in the North of Greece, but this makes little sense since Olympus is not the only place lighted by the sun. It might equally well mean the heavenly abode of the gods towards which the sun throws its rays just as much as to the earth. If we accept the second interpretation, it would show that, like the other pre-Socratics, Empedocles was free from the prejudice of the absolute determination of up and down, right and left, which (along with cold and hot, humid and dry) bedeviled later Greek philosophy. In this interpretation, the sun would be quite free to throw light in all directions: up towards the sky as well as down towards the earth. There are two other short fragments, showing the supremacy of the sun:

> Let me tell you first of the sun as the beginning of all
> by which everything that we now see became apparent.
>   (DK, 31B fr. 38)

and the other fragment consisting of only one line:

> He [the sun] gathering his power together, wanders round the
>   great circle of the sky.   (DK, 31B fr. 41)

Obviously the sun plays a preponderent part in Empedocles' cosmology. It is part and parcel of the original fire, whose explosion, so to say, created the now existent world. It circumscribes our horizon by its orbit round the earth. It makes it possible for us to see all that we see: all the elements in their tangible forms—the earth, the air, the great oceans, and the primeval fire itself.

That is about all that Empedocles tells us in the extant fragments. But we have many reports, from Aristotle on, that he said much more on this subject. One of the most astonishing statements attributed to him is reported by Aristotle (as usual in adverse criticism) to the effect that Empedocles thought we see the sun setting before it actually does. This is the reverse of what we now know to be the case. But it is based on the correct hypothesis that there is a discrepancy between our perception and the actual position of the sun, due to the time the sunlight takes to reach us.

Aristotle was much exercised by the problem of how the light reaches us if it *travels* from the sun to the earth: "Empedocles," he says, "and whoever else holds the same view, are not right in saying that light is traveling from the sun through all that distance; for if it was a question of a small distance, it might escape our notice, but that we do not perceive it during all its course from east to west in the space in between (the sky and the earth) is not reasonable or possible. It is too much to ask us to believe it." (AA, II, vii, 418b) He embroiders on this in another work: "Empedocles says that the light reaches first the space between us and its source, and only later comes to us." (ADS, 6, 446a, 26) We know now that light-waves do in fact travel through space, and that wherever a human eye, or an instrument with the same properties, is placed along their route, it receives the rays and records their image. One other fragment, also consisting of only a single line of verse, raises another issue:

> Night is created by the earth, standing over the source of light.
>
> (DK, 31B fr. 48)

This demonstrates Empedocles' belief that the earth is unattached, hovering in space; held in equilibrium by the swift rotation of the two hemispheres, or, as Anaximander thought, by the equal and opposite attraction of other celestial bodies. He also believed that the sun goes under the earth in its rotation.

Other Observations. Empedocles' cosmology includes some meteorological observations, such as: "The rainbow brings either wind from the sea, or great rain;" (DK, 31B fr. 50) and his reported statement that "Many fires burn under the floor [of the earth]," (DK, 31B fr. 52) by which he explains the intermittent explosions of volcanoes, with which he must have been familiar, living so near Mount Etna.

An attempt was also made by Empedocles to explain the inclination of the earth's axis. Though his explanation is wrong, one cannot help wondering how he knew about the fact of the inclination: "Through the air increasing by the impetus of the sun," says Aëtius, "the poles were filled and the North Pole rose higher than the South Pole; so the whole world got this bias." (DOX, 338)

Two fragments quoted by many commentators have given rise to derision; Both are quoted by Aristotle. The first asserts: "The air penetrates into the earth by long roots;" (DK, 31B fr. 54; AGC, 334a, 5) The other consists of three words: "The sea is a perspiration of the earth." (AML, VI, 446a) To Aristotle, who maintains throughout the absolute distinction of up and down, the first seemed the height of absurdity.

In two other fragments Empedocles presents contradictory pictures. We have already mentioned that he described the moon as consisting of a frozen part of the air, having the consistency of hail. In another fragment he states that "salt is solidified by the warm waves (rays) of the sun." (DK, 31B fr. 56) However, in yet another fragment he states correctly that water evaporates under the warmth of the sun, leaving the solid particles of salt.

The Overall Picture. From the fragments already quoted, and the many comments by later writers, we can form a somewhat vague picture of how Empedoles imagined the periodic creation of the universe. Though in these fragments he only once mentions the four elements as his theoretical foundation, they are always there in the background.

The beginning of each cycle is the havoc created by Strife. In the cosmology this disturbance is traced to its very first root. It is a tremendous explosion, in which the elements are separated from each other. This occurs before the monsters existed and even before there was earth or sky. Air escaped first and surrounded the kernel, the earth. Fire, coming at once after it, rose *through* the air by its nature and remains aloft, exercising a tremendous pressure on the air, which in its turn compresses the earth, making it exude all the humidity that dwells in it—hence the "perspiration" which also gives rise to the seas. This sequence contradicts parts of Empedocles' biology in which he describes the oceans coming before the earth, which emerged gradually by evaporation through the heat of the sun.

Though we have no fragment about the two hemispheres, there are so many reports that the theory must have been asserted. It is an original view, unsupported by any experience. The fact that we constantly face the colder, airy, hemisphere—but mixed with a little fire—requires an effort of the imagination. This explanation assumes that the rotation of the hemispheres involves the earth as well, so that it is always held in the same position in relation to the hemispheres, and faces the airy one; as the moon faces the earth with only one of its surfaces.

We must conclude that the cosmology of Empedocles shows little of the consistency of such other parts of his doctrine as the theory of elements and the theory of sensation. Some of the defects of his cosmology may be due to the very few and short fragments that refer to it. Several apparently absurd statements might have fallen into place if we had more and longer extracts from his exposition building up a more elaborate and coherent picture of his cosmology. Even as it is, several inspiring theories show a grandeur of imagination, and a grasp of fundamental truths. These are: that the sun is at a greater distance from the earth than is the moon; that light *travels* from the sun to the earth and takes a certain time to reach it; that night is caused by he earth interposing its bulk and blocking the rays of the sun. (It is relatively unimportant to this theory whether it is the earth that travels, or the sun which goes under it in his daily circuit.)

It appears that the assertion that the moon is an "alien light" was current in Empedocles' time, but we have no explicit expression of it in the fragments of other philosophers. Further, Empedocles' observation that there are total as well as partial eclipses—the moon "throwing its shadow on the earth as far as its crescent can cover" —is valuable. Plutarch's later astonishing expression about the moon "almost grazing the skin of the earth, and revolving so to stay in its embrace," must surely have been copied from a part of Empedocles' work accessible to him (50–125 A.D.) but lost to us. Finally the theory that the planets are nearer to the earth than are the fixed stars can be inferred from Empedocles' statement that the planets "roam" beneath the crystal dome which forms the outmost boundaries of the sensible world.

In conclusion, although Empedocles' cosmology contains several untenable ideas, it also provides deep insights and, within the bounds of his general theory about the two hemispheres and the visible sun being a reflection of the real one, it might possibly have provided the basis for a further development of astronomical knowledge, free from superstitions and opening a wide field of investigation. Unfortunately, in the words of Aristotle, after Socrates the search for nature's secrets ceased to prevail among philosophers.

8. CONVERSION

Referring to the Sphairos in *On Nature*, Empedocles says:

> But he, on all sides equal and altogether infinite,
> the rounded Sphairos, exultant in surrounding solitude.
> (DK, 31B fr. 28)

And:

> From its back no twin branching arms are swinging;
> it has no feet or swift-moving knees, or sexual organ shaggy,
> It is a sphere, on all sides equal unto itself.   (DK, 31B fr. 29)

In the second work, the *Purifications*, we have again a passage on the Sphairos, repeating some of the above expression word for word, with but one characteristic difference:

> For his limbs are not proudly crowned by a man-like head
> nor do two branching arms from his back swing; he has no feet
> or swift-moving knees, or sexual organ shaggy.
> He's all *one sacred ineffable mind*: by his swift thoughts
> encompassing the entire universe.   (DK, 31B fr. 134)

The similarity of the three passages is so striking that such a great scholar on Empedocles as Ettore Bignone suggests that this third fragment should be included in *On Nature*. (BE, 631ff) Bignone churns over the fragments of *On Nature*, placing them in a quite different order from that of Diels-Kranz, which we follow here. He glosses over the difference of the third fragment from the other two, by stressing the belief of Empedocles that all creatures have feeling and a "share in thought." That is hardly satisfying, since the Sphairos is not a "creature" but the amalgamation of the whole of the universe. Bignone is influenced by his preconception that Empedocles was a mystic from the start, which we contest. In addition to the third fragment just quoted (fragment 134) he also assigns fragments 131-133 to the earlier work, renumbering them 109a-109d.

But the words "one sacred ineffable mind" make all the difference. There is no question in the first work of any consciousness or thought. The Sphairos can only be defined negatively, since it comprises the whole in an inconceivable unity, to which the addition of any qualification would mean a limitation, excluding the opposite qualities. We are reminded of the definition of Spinoza: "Omnis qualification est negatio." And this negation is introduced in the *Purifications*, which tries to retain the Sphairos, but changes its character totally; for by now attributing to it consciousness and thought, Empedocles sets it apart from the elements which make up the whole stuff of the world, and denies it an absolute universality. The Sphairos, the final and initial stage of each cosmic cycle, has gathered unto itself all that there is. There is no sun or moon or thickly wooded earth or living beings or gods. In Fragment 134, the Sphairos traverses "everything" by its swift thoughts. This everything cannot be itself. Hence the Sphairos is here transcendent, outside the world, though it may exist parallel to it, and be contemporaneous with it. This vision of the Sphairos resembles more Xenophanes' conception of the "divine," which is all eyes, all ears, all thought, but does not breathe or perform any other biological functions such as sleeping, eating, etc. If, on the other hand, we accept that the Sphairos, in encompassing everything, surveys its own parts and their order, we are plunged straightway into the theological controversies about the possibility of the Supreme Being having ordered parts, and its relation to them. In any case, the addition of those few words changes totally the significance of the Sphairos and adds to the already inherent contradiction of the expression "all round equal to itself and altogether infinite," by placing the Sphairos outside the existing world, which it is able to survey at one glance. This makes it impossible to accept Bignone's suggestion that fragment 134 formed part of the earlier work.

In addition to many other traits differentiating the two works, this change in Empedocles' conception of the Sphairos leaves little doubt that at some time in his life, and certainly after he had completed *On Nature*, Empedocles experienced a far-reaching change in his views and outlook, amounting to what we would now call a conversion. It is most probable that this happened when he became acquainted with and was received into the inner circle of the Pythagoreans. The school itself had long been dispersed, but its members kept an inner cohesion and could still impose penalties on those who transgressed against their rules, one of which was the prohibition of making certain parts of their doctrine known to the uninitiated. Diogenes Laertius states that, before Empedocles and Philolaos, none of the central theory had been made public. The contradictions about the life of Philolaos are so great and confusing that this information is not much help in dating the adherence of Empedocles to the Pythagorean school. There is also a much-contested story of an alleged letter from Telauges accusing Empedocles of such a transgression. This Telauges, who had become the friend of Empedocles, was a son of Pythagoras; but surely a son of his old age. It is certain, however, that Empedocles absorbed nothing of the mathematical side of the Pythagorean teaching, nor of the mystique of numbers, which ran riot after Pythagoras' disappearance. What interested Empedocles and probably caused his conversion was the Pythagorean teaching of the transmigration of the soul. This presupposed a survival, conscious or unconscious (it makes no difference), of the individual soul, which returns to earth in many forms of life.

Pythagoras himself was known to have maintained that he had already lived many times, and could name four of his incarnations. In the first he was supposed to be the son of the god Ares, who promised to grant him anything he asked for, except immortality. Pythagoras asked to be able to remember his previous incarnations each time that he returned to earth. One of the four names mentioned is Euphorbos, an ally of the Trojans in the Trojan war. He was slain by Menelaus, who brought back Euphorbos' shield to Sparta as part of his war booty. The shield still existed in Pythagoras' time, and though the leather parts of it had rotted, the ivory ornaments survived, and Pythagoras is said to have described them in detail before he had seen the remains of the shield. Diogenes Laertius (DL, VIII, 4) basing himself on Heraklides (VH) mentions one incarnation of Pythagoras as Aethalides, and a more recent one as Hermotimos. Aethalides is also mentioned by Pherekydes. (DK, 7B fr. 8)

It is to be noted that all the incarnations allegedly mentioned by Pythagoras were of men, while Empedocles, faithful to his view of the kinship of all creatures, tells us near the beginning of the *Purifications*:

> For I have at times already been a boy and a girl,
> and a bush and a bird and a mute fish in the salty waves.
>
> (DK, 31B fr. 117)

Another change that occurred in Empedocles' outlook and becomes apparent in the *Purifications* is a deep sense of sin. The Pythagoreans, though imposing severe penalties on transgressions of the rules of the school, did not seem to have been as deeply concerned with sin as Empedocles is in his second work. This leads us to surmise that the Pythagorean doctrine was not the only source of Empedocles' conversion, but that he absorbed other mystical doctrines, not incompatible with it but not explicitly contained in it, such as from the Orphic and other occult sects which were rife in Greater Greece in his time. Also the aspect of Heraclitus' teaching, concerning the "common Nous," from which we all could draw if we only knew how, may have come to the foreground of Empedocles' thought at that period, though he had long been familiar with the Ephesian philosopher's concept of the cosmic cycle.

In some of the fragments of the *Purifications*, though not all, Empedocles still clings to his idea of the historicity of the gods: that is, of their long but not eternal life. One fragment (already quoted in connection with the perigee of Amity's reign) begins:

"There was not among them (the people of that time) Ares, or Zeus the king, (or the god of war-tumult) or Kronos or Poseidon ... but only Kypris was queen," (DK, 31B fr. 28) which seems to show that Empedocles tried very hard to keep the two parts of his theory together; to form one consistent whole.

With great diffidence I venture to suggest that the conception of the spiritualisation of the Sphairos, who has now become "all a sacred mind," may be due to a more remote influence; that of Buddhism. The dates do not clash with this suggestion, for the rise of Buddhism is put at around 500 B.C., half a century before Empedocles' maturity. Nor was it impossible for this new religious movement to percolate through the Persian Empire, which stretched from the western most parts of India to the shores of Asia Minor. Traffic was frequent. The Sphairos would correspond to the Nirvana; the return to human or lower forms of life to Karma; the choice spirits, who sprout up again as "god's immortal" to a Buddha. Empedocles' abhorrence of animal sacrifices, especially bulls and cows, also corresponds to beliefs which are still alive, not only among Buddhists but among those faithful to the older Hindu religion.

The sense of sin, unknown in its present meaning to the Greek world and to the Pythagoreans, was also very strong in the Indian religious as well as in the mystic cults. These analogies may be vague, but they are numerous enough to give a shadow of verisimilitude to an hypothesis which I am aware cannot be substantiated from other sources. Bignone says that Empedocles united in himself the soul of a Greek with that of an Indian. (BE, 21) He even refers to the Buddhist Nirvana. (BE, 182-3) This reference was not however based on an analysis of the relevant fragments; and Bignone (placing Empedocles at the beginning of a Greek medieval period) also compares him to Dante, to Leonardo da Vinci, and to various Christian mystics as well as to the German romantic philosophers, Novalis, Schopenhauer, and a host of others. Such varied comparisons annul each other.

For the Empedocles of *On Nature*, the highest attainment of man is to become merged in the Sphairos and to exist in it as an integral part with no personal memory, no qualifications, no troubles or anxieties. As in Buddhism, the traditional gods are revered, but it would be more in the spirit of Empedocles' first work for them come down and assist in the Gautama's death, rather than to make the Buddha (or Empedocles or whoever has attained human perfection) join them at their "hearth and board." Moreover, as the Nirvana exists side by side with the world of necessity, toil, and repeated incarnations, so now, in the *Purifications*, the Sphairos becomes transcendent, surveying by its swift thought all and everything.

However, the analogies with Buddhism stop here. Empedocles does not envisage the final salvation as an absorption into the universal spirit, but as a deification. After the "souls" have gone through all transmigrations—"bush and bird and mute fish"—and after they have expiated their sins by being thrown from one element to another (each of them spewing the souls out with loathing) those few destined to rise to the highest degree of perfection become "seers, composers of hymns, physicians and leaders of men on this earth; from which they sprout again as gods immortal honored above all," (DK, 31B fr. 146) and, obviously in the same context:

Sharing the hearth and board of the other immortals
untouched by human ills, set apart, not subject to decay.
(DK, 31B fr. 147)

Note that the arts practiced by those perfected human beings are all Empedocles' arts. We have observed that, in his first work, the gods are repeatedly called "long-lived" and "honored above all" but nowhere immortal. In the *Purifications* the word long-lived occurs only once. But, the Olympian gods, whom Empedocles now hopes to join, are a sublimation of ordinary human beings. They quaff nectar, laugh at licentious jokes, bicker about their proteges, envy one another, and intrigue against each other. Eternity among them, as one of them, would be as tedious as in other paradises.

The transmigration of the human soul through all sorts of creatures throughout interminable aeons, implies that beyond the dissolution of the body, made up of combinations of the four ele-

ments, something, consciously or unconsciously, survives for ever.
Whether this "ever" extends only through one cosmic cycle, or
survives through many, is not clear from the existing fragments of
the *Purifications*; though reading through them, one is inclined to
side with the latter view. Gone is the former cheerful acceptance
of the ephemeral character of all living creatures which before
their elements have coalesced and after they have dispersed "were,
and are nothing at all." This change is most apparent in a remarkable fragment, which deserves being quoted in full. What are the
capital sins, whose expiation takes thirty thousand reasons? The
two mentioned in this fragment are bloody sacrifice, which is likened to manslaughter—since the bull and cow may be reincarna-
tions of human beings—and the apparently usual rite of smearing
one's body with their blood. Heraclitus had already derisively
compared this rite to wanting to cleanse oneself from mud by
plunging into mud. (DK, 22B fr. 5)

> There is a law of necessity, an old decree of the gods,
> eternal, bound by the most solemn oaths,
> Whoever fouls his limbs by unwitting involvement in murder
> or swears an oath and then perjures himself,
> the gods, whose lot is a long life, sentence him
> to wander in exile, away from the blessed ones,
> taking on all kinds of shapes of mortal life tormented
> by heavy toil, and to struggle for three times ten thousand
> seasons. For the force of air chases him towards the high
> seas. The sea spews him out towards the threshold of the earth;
> and the earth tosses him towards the sun's shining splendor.
> He in turn hurls him into the whirling of the air.
> Thus one receives him from the other and they all
> loathe him. One of these am I now, a fugitive from the gods
> and a vagrant, having yielded to the enticements of raging Strife.
>   (DK, 31B fr. 115)

I shall not enter into the controversy over three terms in this
fragment: (a) In line 5 I have translated the word of ten rendered by "demons" as the "gods" who have their usual qualification "whose lot is a long life" (demon and god were in ancient
Greek almost synonymous); (b) the "blessed ones" in the next

line; (c) the "gods" from whom the poet considers himself a fugitive and a vagrant. I consider there is very little difference between the three, a matter more of poetic expression than of theology. The "blessed ones" are translated elsewhere as "fair spirits," which means divine beings of a higher grade are banishing a man's soul from a lower realm. I must add that the word "sentence" in line 5 does not occur in the text, but is to be inferred from the nominative of the word "demons" and the accusative of "him." Controversy has also arisen over "the seasons." Leonard equates them with years but the word can also be equally well rendered by seasons of the year, which makes the length of the penalty four times shorter, or by a life's length. Diels-Kranz evades the difficulty by simply transliterating the Greek word, and writing "Horen," which is meaningless.

Despite all these difficulties, the meaning of the fragment is clear: getting involved in murder (which includes slaughtering animals for sacrifice) and perjury are two of the most heinous crimes possible. The culprit, even if he has committed them unwittingly and even if he is already high up in the scale of moral qualities, is cruelly punished and degraded. He must pass through endless transmigrations through all the forms of animate life, roaming the elements, unwanted by any. This horrifying picture of a "lost soul" is not reserved, as in Plato, for the enemies of true philosophy. Empedocles counts himself as one of the sinners; he experiences in himself the horrors of his alleged crime. This absence of the holier-than-thou attitude is the saving grace of a true believer, whatever his faith. And the cry of despair that escapes him in the following fragment corroborates his sincerity:

> Would that a pitiless day had destroyed me
> ere I had thought of polluting my limbs with what my lips have
> tasted!   (DK, 31B fr. 139)

There are many references to a previous life and to an after life in Plato, though they are not consistent with each other. The most beautiful is the picture in Phaedrus. The soul is compared to a charioteer, driving a two-horse winged chariot. He courses through the Empyrean world, which has many cycles, rising to the heavenly visions of the forms of Ideas, and culminating in the Idea of the Good. But the charioteer only occasionally catches a glimpse of these, for although one of his two horses is a noble steed full of spirited valor, the other is a horse of base desires that tends all the time to descend towards the earth. The charioter, having to keep them on an even course round the Empyrean circles, seldom finds a free moment to gaze at the supernatural beauty and harmony of the world of Ideas. Still, the occasional glimpses are in some cases enough. When the time comes for the soul to lose its wings and to return to earth, those who have kept this memory alive become wise and virtuous men, who may hope one day to return to the state from which they have come down.

Other pictures in Plato's work show a malevolence and a thirst for revenge against his, or Socrates' enemies, unworthy of the lofty character customarily attributed to him. There are the torments of hell with which he threatens Kallikles the disciple of Gorgias, in the dialogue of that name; and above all, there is the vision of Er, the Armenian, who, having been slain in battle, remained for ten days under a heap of corpses, and, on being brought out at last and prepared for burial, revived and recounted his adventures among the dead. For he had really died, and had been sent back to earth to enlighten human beings on what was in store for them: torments, such as being skinned alive for ever and ever, or descending to the dark Tartarus, only to emerge after ten thousand years to entreat his victim for pardon, and, if this is not granted it, replunging into that horrible place. These and other ills, plaguing the sinful souls, are given in horrifying detail, testifying to Plato's abundant imagination but not to his humanity. There are nine circles in hell and the lowest but one is allotted to the Sophists. To us this is shocking, for the Sophists did no harm to anyone, and were in their own way real philosophers, taking reality as they perceived it and analyzing the social, political, linguistic, and other phenomena of human life as they presented themselves to them.

Finally, there is the naive conviction of Socrates that, after death, he will continue to converse on justice and virtue and courage with the sages of old, the judges of the Netherworld—Minos,

Rhadamanthys, and Aiakos. But nowhere does Plato's mouthpiece, Socrates, give the slightest hint that he admits to any sin of commission or omission. Nowhere even does he condemn the terrible crimes committed against his country by his boon companions, Alcibiades, Critias, Charmides, and others.

It is quite otherwise with Empedocles. He counts himself amongst the greatest sinners, and he warns repeatedly against bloody sacrifices, maintaining that the bull or cow about to be slaughtered may easily be the mother, father, or son of the man who slits their throat. Several relevant fragments are passionate appeals. We shall refer to two of them here:

> Will you not stop this noisome awful slaughter? Do you not
> see how you tear each other to pieces in the blindness of your
> mind? (DK, 31B fr. 136)

And:

> The father, the utter fool, lifting his knife slits the throat
> of his own dear son, who has changed his form; and the
> bystanders
> offer prayers while he sacrifices. He, mindless of the entreaties
> of the poor victim, having killed him prepares in his princely
> halls a horrible meal. In the same way, a son catches and kills
> his mother, children their father; and having torn the life
> out of them, they consume their kindred flesh.
> (DK, 31B fr. 137)

Do these resemblances to far-away cults imply that we adhere to the school of thought which tends to reduce every single intellectual achievement of the Greeks to the influence of some Oriental tradition or religion? By no means. Controversy over this point raged during the latter half of the 19th century and into the present one, with Edward Zeller—the champion of absolute Greek originality—devoting hundreds of pages in his monumental work, *The Philosophy of the Greeks*, to the refutation of Gladisch and other believers in oriental sources, insisting the Greeks needed no help from other peoples to develop their philosophy. Later, G. Thomson, in *The Early Philosophers*, concedes not one original thought to the Greeks; and Dr. Nestle, editor of Zeller's subsequent editions, has been obliged to mitigate Zeller's absolutism by copious notes, rendered necessary by the discovery of the monuments of Minoan and Mycenean civilisations.

The reply to both schools is fundamentally simple. Of course the Greeks received influences from the surrounding peoples and their culture. If they had not, they would have been obscurantist savages. The influence of the Cretan and in general the Mediterranean civilizations, which extended from Cyprus to Sicily and from the Aegean peoples to the Etruscans, was, in my opinion, perhaps the most decisive of all. The Greeks conquered the lands where those cultures had flourished, intermarried with their inhabitants, examined their shrines, their palaces, and their supreme works of art, heard them speak, copied their script. But the genius of a people can be gauged by the unconscious selection of what they absorb and what they reject; by the way they gradually transform alien elements and make them their own in a form which is unmistakably original, and which adds a new dimension to the human mind and creativeness. Plenty can be said on this concerning art. Specifically Greek elements can immediately be recognized on an Indian vase for instance or in the incomparable "treasury of the Scythians" in the Leningrad Museum, where pieces of similar ornament worked by a native are clearly distinguishable from those of Greek craftsmanship. In philosophy the answer is still simpler: the Greeks were the only people this side of China to develop philosophy as a distinct intellectual discipline, from which all science and all scholarly disciplines of the modern world have "sprouted"—to use Empedocles' expression.

It is probable that the Orphic and similar oriental cults had already been expurgated from their orgiastic and strictly ritual elements by the Pythagoreans before Empedocles came in contact with them, for there is no trace in his work of any such rites as a means of communicating with the divine.

We have already noted how the pre-Greek religion and customs of the Minoan civilization had left a deep imprint on his mind, reinforced by traditions that were still alive among the Sikels, though in a debased form. In the monuments of Crete we have an extreme refinement coupled with a total absence of that glorification of war which was introduced into the Aegean world with the invasion of the Northerners, the Greeks.

The tiny altars of the cult of the Mother Goddess shows conclusively that no sacrifices of animals could have been performed. Hence, we have earlier suggested that the perigee of the cosmic cycle was identified by Empedocles with this already remote period in Mediterranean history when everything was tame and friendly to man and Kypris was conciliated with incense and myrrh "and *painted images* of beasts." (DK, 31B fr. 128) "The trees kept their foliage and bore fruit all the year round." (DK 31B fr. 77/78) This last fragment is transferred by Wilamowitz (WS, 627) from *On Nature* to the *Purifications*, with good reason I believe. We have also noted that there is a sense of two utterly different cultures in Homer's *Odyssey*, whose description of Scheria corresponds very closely with the idyllic descriptions of Empedocles' rule of Amity.

In the *Purifications*, with but a few exceptions like the above fragment and the opening and closing passages, life on earth is painted in the darkest colors. The earth is a joyless place, where Murder and Wrath and a host of smaller malevolent spirits hold away. On entering it "I wept and wailed seeing this unfamiliar place. (DK, 31B fr. 118) Men suffer from shrivelling diseases and all forms of decay

> a place without any charm,
> where Murder and Wrath and a host of other small Destinies
> and shrivelling Diseases, and Rottenness, and all works of man
> run away like water; all these wander about in the dark
> in the fields of Avenging Power.   (DK, 31B fr. 121)

There is also the mysterious fragment: "We came into this roofed-over cave." (DK, 31B fr. 120) Here there is an obvious connection with Plato's comparison of earthly life to existence in a cave, in which only the shadows thrown by the outside light of the true world of Ideas is dimly perceived. That Empedocles considers life on earth a fall (especially for himself) is witnessed by another fragment:

From what great honor and what length of bliss have I fallen
to earth and converse with mortals.   (DK, 31B fr. 119)

Here there sounds again the haughty disdain for common mortality which was so patent throughout the work *On Nature*. Yet
there is a difference. In the earlier work he did not consider he
had come down from any other state. There is no hint of another
sort of existence. Most men are witless and their conceptions are
formed by chance and circumstance, by what they *happen* to
come across; yet they boast of having known the whole etc. In
the *Purifications* his opinion has not changed about the mortals,
but pity and compassion have taken the place of simple contempt:

Oh woe, oh you pitiful race of mortals, of all joy bereft
from what contentious strife were you born, from what depths
     of grief!   (DK, 31B fr. 124)

Such feelings are pushed under the threshold of consciousness in
the first work by Empedocles' elation at his own superiority, that
he alone knows the law of the universe, and that he accepts it will-
ingly, including the prospect of his own disappearance when the
elements composing his body will have separated and dispersed.

Taking the fragments in the order in which they are placed in
The Diels-Kranz's edition, we notice that the *Purifications* begin
on a note of triumph, with a fragment already quoted: "I wander
among you no more a mortal, but as a god immortal . . . crowned
with fillets of gold . . . thousands follow me as I go through the
far-shining cities," asking either for a prophecy or a word of advice to relieve their long-standing sufferings. Immediately after
this, there is a reversal of feeling:

But why do I insist on those things, as if I had achieved
any great thing, in being superior to mortal men, beset
by all kinds of corruption?   (DK, 31B fr. 113)

If these fragments actually followed each other, they show a remarkable consciousness of phenomenon that only great men can
experience. At the moment of their triumph, when they are
recognized and hailed as half-gods by the crowds, a taste of ashes

fills their mouth. What is this triumph worth? What meaning has it for a great writer or for a philosopher, who has struggled throughout his life to express the inexpressible? These honors for which he had striven so long, bitter at the lack of recognition, once achieved, mean very little if anything. "Why do I insist on these things, as if I had achieved any great thing in being superior to mortal men." There is a play of words between "insist" and "being superior": the same verb is used with a different prefix. It is untranslatable, but in Greek it stresses the similarity and the contrast of the two feelings.

There follows the statement that the "onrush of knowledge" is painful and causes envy on the part of small men and then the great fragment of the lost soul of the sinner; "one of them am I now, a fugitive from the gods and a vagrant" (DK, 31B fr. 115), which pictures the very depth of self-abasement. Then the almost cheerful rhythmic account of all the possible transmigrations:

> For I have already at times been a boy and a girl
> and a bush and a bird and a mute fish in the salty waves
> (DK, 31B fr. 117)

There recurs a lament over his fall, then the piece about the "cave" the joyless place with all the malevolent spirits plaguing mankind in the dark fields of avenging power. There follow the cry of pity for mankind, the idyllic description of the time when Zeus and Ares and Kronos "were not yet. . . . ," the passionate warnings against animal sacrifice, and the pessimistic outlook for all men: "suffering from heavy misfortunes, you will never think be free from grievous pains." (DK, 31B fr. 145) Finally, omitting a few small disconnected fragments, some of doubtful authenticity, the *Purifications* end as they began, on a note of triumph. The superior spirits, after going through all forms of living beings, after expiating their sins by much suffering and becoming conscious of the justice of their punishment, reach at last a pinnacle in human life. From that pinnacle, there is no return to the dark cave, to the place of lament, to the torments of wandering through all the elements, all loathing him and spewing him out one to the other. These few, rare men:

In the end they become seers and composers of hymns and
    physicians,
and leaders of men on earth. From these (states) they sprout
up again as gods immortal, honored above all.
(DK, 31B fr. 146)

And:

Sharing the hearth and board of the other immortals,
untouched by human ills, set apart, not subject to decay.
(DK, 31B fr. 147)

After all his strivings, after accepting the dissolution of personality, when the elements composing the body will have dispersed,
after proclaiming the eternal laws of the elements and the forces
and the cosmic cycle, and after he saw himself honored—acclaimed
as a public benefactor, a great poet, a genius—Empedocles feels all
this is not enough. A new longing like a tormenting thirst has entered his breast: he wants immortality. And the only immortality
he, as a Greek, knows is that of the Olympian gods. Whether they
last forever or only one cosmic cycle, and even that not in its
totality, is now immaterial to him. They are always young; they
do not see their skin wrinkle, their teeth and hair fall out, their
joints stiffen. They are not subject to decay. Empedocles has
pushed back from his conscious mind that *change* is a universal
law. He does not consider, as he might have done in his earlier
work, that, in the view of eternity, even the Babylonian year of
262,800 years multiplied by 60 is but a moment. He does not ab-
jure his former beliefs, but the Pythagoreanism (or Buddhism, or
Orphism, or whatever it was) to which he had become converted
promised immortality. Empedocles wanted this immortality to be
personal. He would not be satisfied to become merged in the
"divine inexistence," as a modern Greek poet puts it, of the Nirvana. He would not be satisfied to live on, as Spinoza believed,
as a thought in God, in nature, or in the whole of creation. He
thirsted for personal survival. And how many others have not felt
it bitter to vanish with all that one still could give and all that one
has encompassed in one's thoughts. This would seem another proof
that the *Purifications* is a work of Empedocles' late maturity

(young people do not dread extinction except for fleeting moments); hence the suggestion by Diels-Kranz that the *Purifications* was an early work must certainly be rejected.

Though philosophically somewhat of a step backward, the deep change in Empedocles' attitude, amounting to a conversion, expresses a very genuine human experience and is portrayed in incomparable poetry.

Differences between ON NATURE *and the* PURIFICATIONS

There are five main differences between Empedocles' two great works: In the *Purifications*, the individual soul and personality persists through diverse forms of living beings. ("I have been a boy and a girl and a bush and a bird, and a mute fish.") Men are no longer, as in *On Nature*, a transitory combination of the four elements, dissolving at what witless people call death and not existing before that combination emerged into the light of day. Something over and above that combination—an essence which we could call the soul, though Empedocles does not use the word—survives all forms, sometimes with a dim consciousness of its identity, as when the bull entreats its relative not to slay it. This is a fundamental difference from the conception expressed with such persistence in the work *On Nature*.

The second difference is the introduction of sin, which may or may not be connected with Indian influences. The word now meaning "sin" in modern Greek formerly meant failure, or a fatal mistake, or the disregard of an oracle. In Heraclitus, the elements heavier than fire pay penalties to each other for their tresspasses against the law dictated by the universal Nous. But this did not apply to men. In *On Nature* men are not sinful. When they disperse like smoke they are not held responsible for their acts, they have not to give an account of themselves to any higher power. In the *Purifications*, a commiseration for men has entered Empedocles' heart. He warns and admonishes them against the great sin of offering bloody sacrifices ("Will ye not stop this awful slaughter?") and, supporting other taboos of the Pythagoreans, he cries out: "Miserable, thrice miserable people, keep your hands away from beans" (DK, 31B fr. 141) and "From the leaves of the laurel keep altogether away." (DK, 31B fr. 140) These warnings, passionate and persistent, and the cry "Oh, woe, Oh you pitiful race of mortals (DK, 31B fr. 124) could not possibly have found expression in *On Nature*. They are not inconsistent, though, with Empedocles' earlier view that all living creatures have much in common, that they all breathe in and out, that they all rejoice and grieve, and have a share in thought. The transition is one of feeling rather than of belief. He feels pity, and a duty to warn against sin, though he is not very hopeful that these warnings will have effect:

> Hence, suffering from heavy misfortunes, you will never,
> I think, be free from grievous pains.   (DK, 31B fr. 145)

Another trait of the *Purifications* is the pendulum-like swaying of the philosopher's mood between the extremes of elation, hope, and self-confidence and the opposite extremes of self-abasement and despair. We have noted the contrast between the opening fragment of the *Purifications* which sounds a note of complete triumph—the philosopher wanders among his fellow-citizens "no more a mortal, but like a god immortal," and thousands follow him whenever he appears in the "far-shining cities," needing a prophecy or a word of advice about their manifold ills (DK, 31B fr. 112)—and the immediately following fragment (though we must remember that these are fragments, and we do not know how many verses separated one from the other) in which he chides himself: "as if I had achieved any great thing being superior to the mortals, who are subject to all sorts of decay!" (DK, 31B fr. 113) Then comes the long fragment with the horrifying picture of the lost soul "being tossed by one element to another," loathed by all: "One of these am I now, a fugitive from the gods and a vagrant." The poet feels himself lowest among the low, and it is then that pity and fellow-feeling for the unhappy lot of men on earth enters his heart.

It is needless to continue this enumeration of the contrasting fragments. Most have already been quoted and we have seen that the earth is likened to a dark cavern, and is a joyless place. Man cries and wails when first entering it and innumerable malevolent banes follow him through his life. He totters along amid toil, sickness, and ignorance. Gone is the calm and deep-rooted conviction of *On Nature* that Empedocles alone knew the secrets of the universe. Gone too is the amost joyful acceptance of the transitoriness of human personality. Empedocles has always been deeply conscious of the difficulty of communicating his original and not easily acceptable conception of the world to his disciple Pausanias, and through him to the rest of humanity. He is obliged to use the common language, but he has to twist it round and to squeeze out of the used words a meaning new and fresh, like the juice of a freshly-cut fruit. He manages it with great success in *On Nature*, but he finds it more difficult in the *Purifications* to give a new content to words like "wrath," "murder," "this awful noisome slaughter," etc. He is not misled by the easiness of inventing all those small sprites of annoyance that plague the mortals. He lets himself go in those two fragments, but soon returns to his usual diffidence about the truth, "which is not to be seen with our eyes, nor touched by our hands." (DK, 18B fr. 133) And the remarkable fragment referring to Pythagoras testifies that he has retained the old vigor of his mind and his faith in intellectual power. (DK, 31B fr. 129)

The expression of elation and self-confidence in the opening and closing fragments of the *Purifications* may well have been the reason why the deep-going differences between it and *On Nature* have been to a great extent disregarded.

A fourth major difference between the two works is Empedocles' totally changed attitude towards the gods. He no longer makes a sharp distinction between Kypris (who is not really a goddess, but one of the two cosmic forces—Amity or Love) and the Olympians, whom he treated rather cavalierly in the earlier work. Though they are there always followed by the qualification "the long-living gods, honored above all," he believes them to be temporal phenomena, just as much as the other living beings. In the *Purifications* they are not long-lived but immortal (only in one fragment is the expression "whose lot is a long life" used—DK, 3B fr. 115) and Empedocles now wants to become as immortal as they and to "share their hearth and board." (DK, 31B fr. 147) These gods have sworn an "all-pervading wide oath" about sin and atonement and it is from them that he is now an exile and a vagrant. We have already quoted from Empedocles many invocations to his Muse not to let him be led astray by the honors conferred by men, but to help him utter the deeper truth without fear of favor. There is a similar invocation in the *Purifi-cations*, but its content is very different:

> If thou, immortal Muse, ever wast inclined
> to spend thy care in favor of one of the mortal men,
> be now with me, thy worshipper,
> when I intend to reveal virtuous words about the blessed gods.
>
> (DK, 31B fr. 131)

But this is not all. Wisdom now consists in knowing the truth about the gods. This brings happiness and blessings while, on the other hand, he whose opinion about the gods is dim and erroneous is an unhappy man:

> Blessed is he who has in his possession a wealth of divine thoughts,
> and unhappy the man whose opinion about the gods is darkened.
>
> (DK, 31B fr. 132)

It was not natural for Empedocles to remain long plunged in dismal thoughts and moods, to bewail his exile from the gods, to beat his breast about his sins. The last two fragments of the *Purifications* return to the optimism of its opening, with the difference that they no longer concern life on this earth and the honors paid to wise men or benefactors, but life after death. Presumably, after the long tribulations already described and his genuine contrition, Empedocles feels he is worthy of a blissful and eternal existence. Admittedly very few men achieve this, but he counts himself among these who will be defied and "sprout up again" as gods.

From the point of view of philosophy and theory of knowl-edge, the work of Empedocles' comparatively old age—for he cannot have been more than sixty when he went to Olympia to hear his poem recited—is a come-down from his earlier work

On Nature. Empedocles' conversion may have assuaged his anguish about his own future destiny, but it deprived him of the clear, disinterested eye of the true philosopher. For a man who has seen through the secrets of the universe, as Empedocles claimed to have done, who, though he had not personally experienced them, had "guessed in his mind" the two supreme moments of the cosmic cycle—the ineffable peace of the Sphairos and the reign of Amity from whose loving palms myriads of living forms have poured out, all tame and friendly to each other, "a wonder to behold"—from these concepts to that of the immobility and immutability of the "hearth and board" of the Olympians, who share all the human weaknesses of envy, intrigues, carnal loves, etc., cannot be called an ascent. To be "untouched by decay" is an age-old dream of humanity. But to what purpose? An eternal life without any aim or activity, for a man of Empedocles' temperament, would be, in the long run, intolerable. One cannot even write verses in Paradise.

9. POETRY

We have already mentioned the controversy that raged among the later philosophers, beginning with Aristotle, over the question whether Empedocles was a real poet. Aristotle contradicts himself in a passage from his lost work *De Poetis:* he calls Empedocles Homeric "because he uses metaphor and all the other devices of the poetic trade"; whereas, in a passage in his *Poetica*, he says that "there is nothing in common between Empedocles and Homer except the meter," which is only one of the four characteristics of poetry. Hence Empedocles cannot be considered a true poet. Practically all other commentators agree on this point, except the comparatively obscure Dionysius the Thracian. His commentator (name unknown) repeats the usual adverse criticism of Empedocles' poetry, but Dionysius himself is reported to have said that among those who pursued the austere and difficult harmony (probably thinking of Heraclitus' saying "the hidden harmony is better than the apparent one") Empedocles excelled in epic poetry, Aeschylus in dramatic poetry, and Pindar in lyric poetry. This is high praise indeed.

The Three Levels. Trying to reconcile these contradictions, we have concluded that Empedocles uses the words for his elements in three senses: First, the level of common sense, earth, the ground upon which we tread; air that we breathe; fire that warms us; water that we drink. This level, though of less philosophical importance, inspires him at moments to wonder and admiration over the variety of the forms of living creatures, and hence to expressions like "the immeasurable heights of air," the "life-carrying earth," and others that cannot be called unpoetical.

The second level is that of the elements proper, the primeval stuff out of whose combination and separation in various proportions the whole of the visible world is constituted. This level represents Empedocles' real belief and doctrine. It is on this level that he is inspired to his most original, pithy, and beautiful expressions. But none of the commentators looked for poetry in Empedocles' explanations of the physical world, and almost all concentrated their attention on the third level.

On the third level Empedocles uses much mythological and traditional imaginary and personification, and here he is often impressive and rhetorical but seldom truly poetical as when he says "Zeus, the white splendor," or "Nestis, whose tears bedew humanity" (DK 31B fr. 6) (this last expression I owe to W.E. Leonard), or "firm-clasping Amity." (DK, 31B fr. 19) On this level we also find some fixed metaphors, like the invocation to the gods: "Ye, gods, turn madness away from my tongue, and let through consecrated lips a clear spring flow; and I beseech thee, white-armed virgin Muse, send me in Piety's well-reined chariot what is meet for ephemeral men to hear; nor let thyself be compelled by the wreaths of praise of mortal men to say more than is pious" (DK, 31B fr. 3)

This kind of rhetorical poetry, using all the trite, traditional arsenal of poetic expressions, white-armed virgin, well-reined chariot, and the like, is certainly not real, original poetry. Later in the same fragment, it is obvious that Empedocles is warning himself, or his disciple, not the muse. This lack of consistency is not remarked upon by anyone. (Sextus Empiricus takes it as a chiding to those who promise more knowledge than is carried by each sense-organ!) On this level we have also the single verse "sharp-arrowed sun and mild-shining moon." (DK, 31B fr. 40) This kind of poetry (though Empedocles has occasional flashes of originality) had been worked to death in the Homeric cycle. It reaches at times an insufferably high pitch in the *Purifications*, the work which caused such a great stir and bewilderment when performed by the professional rhapsode Cleomenes at Olympia. Yet certain parts of it are really gripping because of the depth and sincerity of the feeling behind them, and Empedocles' description of the tribulations of the sinful soul althrough aeons of trans-migrations—"tossed," "hurled," and "spewed" from one element to the other—is not paralleled in any other of the great poets of his period. Two cries wrung from him are great poetry:

Would that a pitiless day had destroyed me
ere I had thought of polluting my limbs with what my lips have
        tasted!   (DK, 31B fr. 139)

Oh woe, you pitiful race of mortals, of all joy bereft!
From what contentious Strife were you born,
from what depths of grief!   (DK, 31B fr. 124)

If judgments on Empedocles' poetry were to be based on the verbal fireworks we have mentioned—and the fact that they have been preserved shows that they impressed ancient posterity—we could only have said that Empedocles knew how to use all the traditional forms of poetry, that he could produce impressive combinations of them, and that on certain occasions he showed deep insight. But the real poetry of Empedocles lies in the fragments expounding his doctrine: his conception of the elements as the real basis of existence; the laws of their changes; the nothingness of human and animal life as compared with the awful majesty of the Sphairos; the description of how mortal beings come into being and then vanish like smoke. And again, tinged with a deep consciousness of ephemeral being, his delight in forms and colors; in the variety of animals and plants; in the splendor of the sun and moon and mountains, where lions lay themselves on the ground and sleep; in the sea, where Amity "leads the voiceless throng of profusely-spawning fish." These are his own visions and convictions, and he devotes endless care and ability to the expression of every detail. Shining intuitions light the abstract thoughts and flash in unforgettable utterances—cries torn out of his mental toil and concentration. Coherence and audacity, pithiness and clarity, are combined.

We may reserve judgment on the details of his theory; but, while we are immersed in it, it carries conviction and compels our admiration. The abstract becomes concrete through the highest poetry. We long for the Sphairos to end the tribulations of this life, and then again we marvel with the poet at the myriads of living forms, so different in shape and color. We almost submit to the ineluctable law of the elements and to the prospect of going up like smoke at our death.

Empedocles is conscious that his vision is unique, and this is the reason why he repeats many passages in a slightly different form, saying two or three times: "I shall now retrace my steps and let my words follow each other"; things he has discovered come out more clearly, each time slightly different and enhanced:

> And of a sudden they become mortal, those previously wont to
> be immortal.   (DK, 31B fr. 35)

Wandering far from their own kind, the elements mix with each other:

> and when having come together in the proper mixture, they rise
> to the light in the shape of a man, or of beasts living in the wild,
> or as bushes or birds, then people call it birth.
>   (DK, 31B fr. 9)

And the same contradiction lies at the base of all creation:

> Thus they come into being and their life is not long their own,
> but in so far as they never stop changing throughout
> in so far they are forever immovable in a circle.
>   (DK, 31B fr. 17)

The same thought in a slightly different form:

> They (the elements) are forever themselves; but, running
> through each other, they become at times different,
> yet are forever and ever the same.   (DK, 31B fr. 17)

Empedocles admits the repetitiveness which Aristotle finds so objectionable, but with a difference:

I shall now retrace my steps and come back to my song's
   beginning,
to what I said before, letting new words flow
from those I previously uttered.   (DK, 31B fr. 35)

The Larger Fragments. In the three longer descriptive fragments, that of the comparison to the painters, that of the lantern,
and that of the clepsydra, Empedocles' poetic inspiration adds a
concrete touch, a sense of immediate reality to what he wishes
to convey. And they *tally*—an essential characteristic all good
similes or concrete images of abstract things. All Homeric descriptions of this kind tally, each point of the concrete image corresponding to another point in the real happening he describes.

In the first of these long fragments Empedocles is not content
to talk simply about "the painter." They are "men well versed in
their art, knowledgeable by the force of their mind." They mix
their colors in their palms (an echo of Aphrodite here) inspired
by Harmony—"here a little more, there a little less"—and produce
shapes similar to all things existing: "trees and buildings and men
and women, wild beasts and birds and water-nurtured fish, and
long-lived gods, honored above all." (DK, 31B fr. 23)

In the comparison of our eyes to a lantern, "a man intending to
set forth in the wintry night prepares himself a lantern, a light of
burning fire, whose sides hinder the rush of all winds, and scatter
their breath, while the fire penetrates outside, insofar as it is finer
and more tenuous. . . . in like fashion was the eternal fire fenced
round and hidden in finest veils enclosing the round pupil; the
veils being pierced all over by passages divinely wrought." (DK,
31B, fr. 84)

In similar detail he compares inhaling and exhaling breath with
the working of the clepsydra: "as when a young girl, playing
with a water-clock of gleaming bronze, so long as by her tender
hand the pipe is closed, and her delicate finger is plunged in and
made wet by the silvery water." (DK, 31B, fr. 100)

In these similes, the details could be said to be gratuitous. The
hand might just as well have been horny and rough; the night
into which the man is setting forth need not have been wintry;

the painters need not have been described as men "knowledgeable by the force of their mind." The theoretical content of each simile would have been the same, but it would not imprint itself on our mind. We would not *see* the man lighting his lantern, the painters kneading their colors in their sensitive hands, intent on "a little more here, a little less there," nor feel, with the girl, the water gurgling against her finger, rushing to get out but hindered by her "tender hand." These qualifications are not ornamental touches added a posteriori. They are part of the way in which the philosopher-poet conceived and visualized his subject. In these, as in so many other original expressions, Empedocles shows himself a poet who cannot help being one; a genuine poet who thinks in images, whose content, instead of the diffuse and often contradictory imagery of minor poets, conveys the result of deep pondering and a systematic conception of the universe.

And it is not only in beautiful imagery that his poetic genius reveals itself: he is equally impressive in the weird and the horrible, in picturing the primeval monsters which peopled the world before Harmony or Love entered it to create an ordered cosmos out of the havoc wrought by Strife. Empedocles' single limbs wandering unattached can not be an accurate description of what really occurred in the prehistoric days. They are nevertheless indicative of the utter disorder of living matter, tottering without direction in the prevailing Chaos,

> in which many a head grew without a neck, and naked arms
> wandered about without supporting shoulders,
> and eyes bereft of a forehead. (DK, 31B fr. 57)

And

> [creatures] consisting of one limb still wandered about.
> (DK, 31B fr. 58)

The sexes were separated, the men's and the pitiful women's, after the lumpy bisexual creatures, bereft of speech and of love's urge and desire, had been separated by the fire surging upwards. The same theory is expounded at length—minus the fire's action—by Aristophanes in Plato's *Symposium*. Love is there explained as the longing of each half to be reunited with its other half. Here we find echoes of Empedocles' ideas, as also of his half-verse, "we came into this roofed-over cave," (DK, 31B fr. 120) which is the earthly world. One cannot help admiring Empedocles' arbitrary definitions of what distinguishes man from all other animals: his capacity for love's desires and fulfilment and for articulate speech.

The Poetry of the Purifications. In the *Purifications*, the poetry is a mixture (as far as can be assessed from the fewer fragments we have than of the earlier work), a motley of the two kinds of poetry we were able to discern in *On Nature*. There is the verbal, rhetorical, highly skillful manipulation of words, using traditional names and adjectives, and also the poetry of deep-felt conviction. Several examples of the rhetorical kind have already been given; others are the heapings of names of the various little banes of Moiras (Slothful and Quick, Silent and Prattling, etc.). In the *Purifications*, the conviction and pain out of which all true poetry is born is not speculative but moral in character. It is more personal, it introduces us to the extremes of elation and depression of a highly-strung personality. It oscillates sharply between self-assertion and humility. Empedocles' newly-acquired faith in the transmigration of the soul and in the expiation of sin makes him abase himself as he becomes aware that before his conversion he has, along with most mortals, committed the capital sin of taking part in animal sacrifices. Empedocles feels this so deeply that the cry escapes him: "Would that a pitiless day had destroyed me, ere I had thought of polluting my limbs with what my lips have tasted!" (DK, 31B fr. 139) He warns people at large: "Don't you see how you tear each other to pieces?" (DK, 31B, fr. 136) The longest fragment, which describes the soul's expiation through aeons of wandering from one element to the other all loathing him (already quoted) reveals vividly a man absolutely convinced of the truth of what he says. The doctrine of the transmigration of the soul seems to have sunk more deeply into Empedocles than into most of the Pythagoreans.

We have seen that the first fragment of the *Purifications* (DK, 31B, fr. 112) seems like a natural sequence to the last of *On*

Nature, (DK, 31B, fr. 111) in which he promised his disciple
power over nature, medicines to stay old age, and power to raise
people from the dead. In the opening fragment of the *Purifications*
he arrogates these powers to himself, describing his progress
through far-shining cities with throngs following him everywhere,
requesting a prophecy or advice on their ailments. It is an hour
of triumph such as he must have dreamt of for years: a panhellenic
recognition of his supremacy. And suddenly he realizes that all
his achievements are vain and his boasting small-minded:

> Why do I insist on these things, as if I had achieved
> any great thing in being superior to mortal men, subject
> to all kinds of decay?   (DK, 31B, fr. 113)

This is a sign of real greatness, and a psychological phenomenon
which only prominent men can experience: to recognize wordly
success as a brittle thing, unworthy of the toil and ambition
bestowed on it; perhaps to become aware that one is acclaimed
for the wrong reason (for the not quite poetical verses Empedocles had let them hear at Olympia?). If I were to make so bold
as to change the order of the fragments—as many others have
done—I would place this fragment, and the next one, nearer the
end of the work. Empedocles knows the labor he has devoted to
his work, but he senses around him astonishment rather than admiration, envy rather than devotion:

> toilsome and heavy and a cause of envy to men is
> the onrush of knowledge into their minds   (DK, 31B, fr. 114)

Intellectual effort brings no reward, it is a fatal advantage. He
feels that faith in his own insight, the result of so long a process
of thought and research, is like being possessed by a power above
the capacities of the common run of men: but a possession that he
would not forsake for anything. The "toilsome onrush of knowledge into the mind" is, I think, a capital poetical find. The description of the Sage (Pythagoras) in a later fragment leaves us no
doubt that despite everything—the "joyless place," the dark
"roofed-over cave," the many dooms and banes, and the long

process of expiation of sin through thousands of years—it is worth-while achieving this rare quality:

> There was a man among them . . . who, when he tensed his whole
> intellectual power, could easily *see* each one of the totality
> of things easier than ten men in twenty lives.
>
> (DK, 31B, fr. 129)

That he also had reached that summit seemed to him certain and a source of inner contentment, even of boasting, in the earlier work. Now, it flashes by at times, but it is not enough. What he now wants is immortality, whether during one cosmic cycle, or during many successive ones. The two lines:

> for I have at times already been a boy and a girl and a bush
> and a bird and a mute fish in the salty waves
>
> (DK, 31B, fr. 117)

sound almost triumphant. He has gone through all possible forms of living beings; he has paid dearly for his sin and has reached the summit from which men "sprout up again" as gods immortal, "sharing the hearth and board of the other immortals, untouched by human ills, not subject to decay."

The *Purifications* end on that note, except for a few isolated words cited by later commentators. It is not impossible to recon-cile this conception with the one in *On Nature*. The cosmic cycle is very long. During all that time many of the Olympians are untouched by decay and, for the moment, Empedocles seems to have forgotten the Sphairos: he is too concentrated on his own destiny. When the time comes, the impersonal and ineffable mind of the Sphairos will take care of him, absorbing him like every-thing else.

The contradictions between the two works may thus be evened out. They are contradictions only on the surface. The poetic genius of Empedocles has shown us the way in which he thought and felt. Perhaps I have turned the fragments too much around, perhaps I have seen more biographical and psychological details in the verses of the *Purifications* than the work really includes. But that also is the effect of great poetry: to show one a superior personality going through all phases of research, speculation, and effort to overcome the obvious and common sense view; and later the illumination by a faith he has absorbed so deeply that he can even betray it.

Conclusion. In Empedocles' poetry, we must reject the sheer rhetorical fireworks of the enumeration of the banes, the exhortations to his muse and to the gods to let only pure words flow from his consecrated lips, and all other verses of this kind. They may have impressed his contemporaries and the later commentators, but these are precisely the words that he uttered for "the many." When one reviews all the existing fragments, one finds there are not too many such passages.

In the case of most of the fragments of *On Nature* and those from the *Purifications* which express genuine contrition, genuine pity for miserable mortals, real elation at his own powers, and real abhorrence for what he now considers capital sins, we can accept Dionysius the Thracian's evaluation of Empedocles as a poet on a par with Aeschylus and Pindar. For the test of real poetry is that it does not go stale with repetition but opens up new horizons at each new reading.

INDEX

AA, see *De Anima* (Aristotle)

Abdera, 21, 24

AC, see *DeCaelo* (Aristotle)

Achaean 9

Achilles 101

Adam xv

ADP, see *DePoetis* (Aristotle)

Adversus Mathematicos (Sextus Empiricus) 3

ADR, see *De Respiratione* (Aristotle)

ADS, see *De Sensu* (Aristotle)

Aegean 8, 9, 35, 61, 62, 126, 127

Aelian, Aelianos (Claudius) 3, 90

Aeschylus 136, 145

Aethalides 119

Aëtius, also see *Doxographi Graeci* 3, 47, 51, 70, 95, 96, 109, 110, 113

Aetna, Mount vi, 16, 17, 112

AGC, see *De Generatione et Corruptione* (Aristotle)

Agrigentum 7

Aiakos 124

Aidoneus 44

Air x, xiii, 31, 41, 42, 43, 44, 45, 46, 47, 51, 68, 92, 102, 107, 108, 111, 113, 122, 136, 137

Akragas 7, 8, 9, 10, 11, 13, 15, 17, 19, 21, 62

Alcibiades 125

Alcmeon 79, 81, 83, 98

Alexander the Great 22

Alexander the Knowledgeable 3

Alexandria, Alexandrine 3, 4, 5, 6, 51f.

Alice Through The Looking Glass (Lewis Carroll) vi, vii

Amity xii, xiii, 48, 49, 50, 52, 55, 56, 59, 60, 62, 63, 65, 66, 68, 69, 71, 72, 77, 82, 86, 100, 102, 103, 119, 124, 133, 135, 137, 138

AML, see *Meteorologia* (Aristotle)

Among School Children (W. B. Yeats) ix

AMP, see *Metaphysica* (Aristotle)

Anaxagoras 1, 6, 16, 34, 70, 106, 109

Anaximander 14, 23, 24, 25, 41, 42, 112

Anaximines 24, 41, 42

Anchites 21

Animals/Beasts 48, 56, 58, 60, 61, 63, 75, 79, 83, 95, 96, 98, 101, 127, 140, 142

AP, see *Poetica* (Aristotle)

APA, see *De Partibus Animalium* (Aristotle)

Aphrodite 48, 55, 59, 60, 67, 68, 70, 77, 86, 100, 104

Apollo 14

Apollodorus 25

AR, see *Rhetorica* (Aristotle)

Archinomos 9, 10

Ares 59, 118, 120, 129

Arete 61

Aristophanes 141

Aristotle, Aristotelian ix, xvii, 2, 4, 6, 8, 12, 14, 16, 25, 26, 27, 28, 30, 31, 40, 42, 43, 44, 45, 46, 50, 69, 70, 75, 76, 78, 87, 90, 91, 94, 96, 97, 98, 99, 106, 109, 111, 112, 113, 115, 136, 139

Arnold, Matthew, *Empedocles on Aetna* vi, 1, 20

Art of Grammar, The (Dionysius the Thracian) 5

Artemis 18, 35

Aryan 62

Asclepios, Asclepiad 21

ASE, see *Sophistici Elenchi* (Aristotle)

Asia Minor 22, 25, 31, 32, 35, 120

Assyria, Assyrian 23, 106

Astronomy, Astronomical 40, 42, 58, 106, 115

Athena 61
Athens, Athenian 4, 8, 20, 21, 22, 23, 24, 26, 109
Attic, Attica 6, 17, 18

Babylonia, Babylon 10, 39, 57, 65, 106, 107, 130
Banquets 10, 13, 15, 16, 18
Baudelaire xiii
BE, see *Empedocle* (E. Bignone)
Beasts, see Animals
Bignone, Ettore xvii, 1, 116, 117, 118, 120
Biologist, Biology 20, 62, 92, 94, 96, 97, 98, 101
Birds 48, 56, 83, 99, 100, 119, 121, 129, 131, 140, 144
Boussoulas, L. N. 56
Britain 61
Buddhism xv, 120, 121, 130
Bull 16, 30, 60, 63, 99, 120, 122, 125, 131
Burnt Norton x, xi, xii
Byzantine 5

Cadmus 23, 40
Carroll, Lewis vi
Carthage, Carthaginian 7, 21, 22
Chaldean Priests 106
Charmides 125
China 126
Christianity, Christian Thought xii, 3, 4, 6, 120
Circulation (of the blood) 92, 98
Clemens of Alexandria, also see *Doxographi Graeci* 4, 108
Cleomenes 13, 138
Clepsydra (water-clock) 92, 140
CMG, see *Corpus Medicorum Graecorum*
Colchis 18
Collection of Physical Opinions (Aëtius) 3
Comte, Auguste 105
Conversion 14, 63, 118, 135, 142
Corinth 24

Corpus Medicorum Graecorum xvii, 51
Corybantes 61
Cosmic Cycle, The 30, 31, 45, 49, 52, 53, 54, 57, 62, 64, 65, 66, 89, 101, 102, 103, 104, 117, 119, 122, 127, 130, 135
Cosmology 33, 106, 107, 111, 113, 114, 115
Crates 35
Creatures vii, 46, 47, 49, 50, 52, 54, 58, 59, 60, 62, 65, 78, 79, 86, 92, 97, 101, 104, 116, 122, 132, 141
Crete, Cretan 7, 8, 61, 62, 126
Critias 23, 125
Croton 35, 38
Crump, Marjorie xiii
CW, see *Stobaeus, Ioannis* (C. Wachsmuth)
Cynics 2, 42
Cyprus 126
Cyrenaica 23

Danaids 64f
Dante 120
Darwin, Charles (Darwinism) x, 62, 101
Da Vinci, Leonardo 120
DCV, see *De Compositione Verborum* (Dionysius the Thracian)
De Abstinentia (Porphyry) 61
De Anima (Aristotle) xvii, 87, 97, 112
De Caelo (Aristotle) xvii, 2, 70, 106
De Compositione Verborum (Dionysius the Thracian) xvii, 28
De facie in orbe lunae (Plutarch) xvii, 5, 108, 110, 114
De Fortuna Alexandri (Plutarch) xvii, 99
De Genit. (Hippocrates) 95
De Generatione et Corruptione (Aristotle) xvii, 2, 45, 70, 76, 78, 113
De Heraclides (O. Voss) xvii, 9, 10, 11, 16, 119
De Natura Animalium (Aelian) 90

De Partibus Animalium (Aristotle) xvii, 97

De Pietate (Theophrastus) 61

De Placitis Philosophorum (Aëtius) 47

De Poetis (Aristotle) xvii, 2, 8, 45, 136

De Respiratione (Aristotle) xvii, 2, 98

De Sensu (Aristotle/Theophrastus) xvii, 2, 75, 78, 112

Death of Empedocles, The (Hölderlin) 13, 20

Demeter 101

Democritus, and see *Die Fragmente der Vorsokratiker* 21, 23, 24, 40, 90

Diels, H. xvii, 5, 14, 64f, 67f, 116, 123, 128, 131

Dike 32, 34

Dionysian Mysteries 106

Dionysius of Syracuse 22

Dionysius the Thracian 5, 28, 136, 145

Dionysius the younger 33

Dionysus (the God) 34, 44, 96

DK, see *Die Fragmente der Vorsokratiker* (Diels-Kranz)

DL, see *History of Philosophers* (Diogenes Laertius)

Doric, Dorian 8, 9, 26, 62

Dostoevsky xiii

Double Truth vi, vii, xii, xiii, 45, 59, 68, 81

DOX, see *Doxographi Graeci* (Diels)

Doxographi Graeci (Diels) xvii, 5, 41, 42, 47, 51, 70, 71, 75, 78, 79, 95, 108, 109, 110, 112

Dry Salvages x

Early Philosophers, The (G. Thomson) 125

Earth x, xiii, 31, 42, 44, 45, 47, 50, 51, 58, 59, 68, 80, 92, 100, 102, 111, 112, 113, 114, 117, 122, 136, 137

East Coker x, xi, xiv

Effluvia 38, 73, 74, 78, 82

Egypt, Egyptian 5, 10, 23, 35, 39, 42, 106

Eleatic School, Elea 10, 22, 25, 26, 27, 30, 31, 32, 33, 34, 38, 43, 58

Elements 31, 32, 34, 39, 41, 42, 43, 45, 46, 47, 48, 49, 50, 51, 52, 54, 55, 56, 57, 58, 59, 62, 65, 66, 69, 70, 73, 77, 79, 80, 81, 82, 83, 86, 87, 89, 90, 91, 92, 101, 102, 103, 104, 108, 111, 113, 114, 117, 121, 122, 123, 129, 130, 131, 132, 136, 137, 138, 139, 142.

Eliot, T. S. vi, viii, xii, xiii, xiv, xv

Emotion of Multitude, The (W. B. Yeats) xiii

Empedocle (E. Bignone) xvii, 116, 120

Empedocle, ou l'age de la haine (Romain Rolland) 20

Empedocles on Aetna (Matthew Arnold) 20

Empiricus, Sextus 3, 137

Enneads 4

Epaminondas 36

Ephesus 31, 33, 35, 39, 42

Epicureans 2

Epyllion xiii

Epyllion From Theocritus to Ovid, The (M. Crump) xii

Er, the Armenian 124

Eteocretans 61

Etruscans 126

Euclid vi

Euphorbus 119

Eustathius 107

Exainetos 10

Explanation (Suidas) 25

Eye 76, 77, 78, 103, 117, 133, 140, 144

Favorinus 4, 9

FGH, see *Fragmente der Griechischen Historiker*, ed. Jacobs

FHG, see *Fragmenta Historicum Graecum*, ed. C. Miller

Finnegan's Wake vii

Fire x, xiii, 31, 32, 43, 44, 45, 46, 47, 50, 58, 59, 76, 77, 92, 100, 101, 102, 107, 108, 111, 113, 114, 136, 140

Fish 48, 56, 59, 90, 99, 103, 119, 121, 129, 131

Forces 44, 45, 47, 48, 50, 52, 56, 67, 69, 70, 77, 81, 86, 87; 89, 103, 133

Four Quartets viii, x, xi, xii, xiv

Die Fragmente der Vorsokratiker:
Diels xvii, 14, 18, 20, 28, 29, 30, 33, 34, 40, 42, 44, 45, 47, 48, 49, 50, 51, 52, 53, 54, 55, 56, 57, 58, 60, 63, 64, 67, 69, 73, 74, 75, 76, 77, 79, 80, 81, 83, 84, 85, 87, 88, 89, 90, 99, 100, 101, 102, 104, 107, 109, 111, 112, 113, 116, 119, 120, 121, 122, 123, 125, 127, 128, 129, 130, 133, 134, 137, 138, 139, 140, 142, 143, 144

31 B : Empedocles
31 B fr. 2 : 20, 46, 54, 73, 74, 87
31 B fr. 3 : 81, 84, 88, 137
31 B fr. 4 : 89
31 B fr. 6 : 58, 137
31 B fr. 9 : 55, 83, 139
31 B fr. 12 : 27
31 B fr. 14 : 27, 83
31 B fr. 15 : 27, 54, 90
31 B fr. 16 : 67, 104
31 B fr. 17 : 29, 45, 47, 51, 55, 56, 67, 68, 69, 88, 102, 139
31 B fr. 19 : 137
31 B fr. 21 : 34, 48, 51, 56, 102
31 B fr. 23 : 48, 140
31 B fr. 24 : 83
31 B fr. 26 : 51, 102
31 B fr. 27 : 29, 52, 53, 58
31 B fr. 28 : 29, 52, 53, 116
31 B : fr. 29 : 30, 53, 116
31 B fr. 31, 32 : 100
31 B fr. 35 : 50, 69, 70, 139, 140
31 B fr. 38 : 80
31 B fr. 38 : 111
31 B fr. 39 : 28
31 B fr. 40 : 107, 137
31 B fr. 41 : 111
31 B fr. 42 : 109
31 B fr. 44 : 111
31 B fr. 45 : 108, 109

31 B fr. 47 : 109
31 B fr. 48 : 112
31 B fr. 50 : 112
31 B fr. 52 : 112
31 B fr. 53 : 102
31 B fr. 54 : 113
31 B fr. 56 : 113
31 B fr. 57 : 49, 141
31 B fr. 58 : 141
31 B fr. 60 : 49
31 B fr. 61 : 49
31 B fr. 62 : 100
31 B fr. 64 : 100
31 B fr. 71 : 60, 86
31 B fr. 73 : 60, 100
31 B fr. 79 : 100
31 B fr. 82 : 51, 99
31 B fr. 83 : 99
31 B fr. 84 : 76, 140
31 B fr. 85 : 77
31 B fr. 86 : 77
31 B fr. 87 : 77
31 B fr. 88 : 77
31 B fr. 89 : 91
31 B fr. 90: 80
31 B fr. 92 : 50
31 B fr. 95 : 101
31 B fr. 98 : 90, 102
31 B fr. 99 : 78
31 B fr. 100 : 93, 94, 140
31 B fr. 101 : 75
31 B fr. 103 : 86
31 B fr. 105 : 79
31 B fr. 108 : 87
31 B fr. 109 : 27, 80
31 B fr. 110 : 85, 88
31 B fr. 111:19, 91, 104, 143
31 B fr. 112 : 14, 17, 19, 132, 142
31 B fr. 113 : 128, 132, 143
31 B fr. 114 : 89, 143
31 B fr. 115 : 20, 52, 122, 128, 133
31 B fr. 116 : 52, 63
31 B fr. 117 : 119, 129, 144
31 B fr. 118 : 63, 127
31 B fr. 119 : 128

31 B fr. 120 : 127, 142
31 B fr. 121 : 64, 127
31 B fr. 122 : 64
31 B fr. 123 : 64
31 B fr. 124 : 128, 132, 138
31 B fr. 128 : 60, 63, 149
31 B fr. 129 : 38, 90, 133, 144
31 B fr. 130 : 127
31 B fr. 131 : 84, 134
31 B fr. 132 : 134
31 B fr. 133 : 133
31 B fr. 134 : 116, 117
31 B fr. 136 : 63, 125, 142
31 B fr. 137 : 64, 125
31 B fr. 139 : 123, 138, 142
31 B fr. 140 : 132
31 B fr. 141 : 132
31 B fr. 145 : 129, 132
31 B fr. 146 : 17, 121, 130
31 B fr. 147 : 121, 130, 133

Fragmenta Historicum Graecum (ed. C. Miller) xvii, 5, 9, 10, 14, 15, 16
Fragmente der Griechischen Historiker (ed. Jacoby) xvii, 5, 9, 10, 11, 12, 23, 25, 36, 40
Freud, Sigmund ix

Galen 51, 70, 98
Ganymede 18
Gela 7, 8, 11, 21, 62
Goethe 7
Gerontion xiv
Gladisch 125
Golden Sayings of Pythagoras (Hierocles) 3
Gorgias, of Leontini 24, 26, 124
Great World Order, The (Democritus) 24
Greater Greece 22, 23, 24, 35, 119
Gylippus 8
Gynaecology (Seranos) 95
Hades 34
Hamlet x
Harmony, Harmonius 33, 48, 50, 59,

64, 65, 71, 103, 104, 140, 141
Hatred, Hate 48, 57, 61, 66, 67, 71, 80
HE, see Herodotus
Hecataeus 23, 41, 42
Hedgehog 99, 103
Hegel, Hegelian 32
Hera 44
Heraclides, Heraklides 9, 10, 12, 16, 119
Heraclitus, also see *Die Fragmente der Vorsokratiker* xii, 6, 10, 31, 32, 33, 34, 35, 38, 40, 42, 44, 45, 47, 50, 57, 63, 67, 82, 84, 90, 119, 122, 131, 136
Hermotimus 119
Herodotus xvii, 11, 13, 23, 40, 41
Hesiod 30, 33, 106
Hierocles 3
Hippobotus 70
Hippocrates, Hippocratic, Hippocratean 18, 31, 51, 95, 98
Hippolytus 44, 51
Hipponicus, of Metapontium 42
History of All Sorts (Favorinus) 4
History of Philosophers (Diogenes Laertius) xvii, 2, 11, 13, 15, 16, 25, 42, 62, 70, 71, 108, 119
History of the Philosophers (Porphyry) 4
Hölderlin 1, 13, 20
Homer, Homeric viii, 2, 28, 30, 44, 84, 127, 136, 137, 140
Humpty Dumpty vi, vii, viii, xiv
Hypocrite lecteur mon semblable, mon frere (Baudelaire) xiii

Iamblichus 4
Immobile, Immobility 26, 28, 30, 31, 33, 34, 41, 53, 57, 135
Immortality, Immortal 4, 14, 17, 18, 19, 23, 37, 50, 54, 56, 69, 97, 118, 121, 128, 130, 132, 133, 134, 139, 144
India, Indian 23, 35, 39, 120, 126, 131
Infinite 28, 30, 41, 42, 43, 52, 118
Ionic, Ionian, Ionia 6, 9, 22, 23, 24
Iphigenia 18

Isis 5
Italy, Italian 10, 13, 15, 17, 22, 23, 24, 35

Joyce, James vii, viii

Kallikles 124
Karma 120
Kea 24
King 12, 18, 32
Knowledge 74, 81, 82, 83, 85, 86, 87, 88, 89, 90, 91, 129, 143
Kolophon 28, 42
Kranz, Walther xvii, 14, 64f, 67f, 116, 123, 128, 131
Kronos 60, 120, 129
Kylon 36
Kypris 48, 59, 60, 64, 103, 120, 127, 133

Laertes 2
Laertius, Diogenes 2, 15, 16, 17, 42, 70, 108, 119
Lampsacus 16
Lantern 76, 94, 130
Lear, King x
Leningrad 126
Leonard, W. E. 30, 44, 52, 64, 80, 123, 137
Leontini 24, 26
Little Gdiding x, xiv
Logos xii, 32, 33, 88
Love vi, x, xi, 46, 48, 51, 55, 62, 66, 68, 71, 80, 103, 104, 133, 141
Lydia, Lydian 40
Lysis 36

Manethos 42
Mars 59
McLuhan, J. Marshall vi
Megara 17, 23, 43
Melissos 22
Metaphysica (Aristotle) xvii, 2, 30, 42, 45, 50, 70, 87, 97
Memorabilia (Favorinus) 9
Menelaus 119

Messina 16
Metapontium 36, 38, 42
Meteorologica (Aristotle) xvii, 113
Meteorologica (Theophrastus) 2
Meton 9
Miletus, Milesian 10, 14, 23, 24, 25, 40, 42, 108
Minoan 61, 126
Minos 124
Mixture 1, 39, 48, 49, 51, 54, 56, 57, 69, 139
Monism, Monist 26, 39, 42
Monsters, Monstrous Creatures, Monstrosities vii, 49, 52, 56, 59, 62, 63, 65, 67, 100, 101, 113
Moon 5, 107, 108, 109, 110, 113, 117, 137
Mother Goddess 61, 127
Morphology 98, 99, 102
Movement 25, 27, 28, 31, 34, 41, 42, 57, 108
Mycenean 126

Nauck, A. 36
Nausicaa 61
Neanthes 5, 9, 10, 36
Necessity 46, 52, 63, 66
Neikos 48
Neilos 23
Neoplatonists 3, 4, 36, 61
Nestis 44, 137
Nestle 126
Netherworld 19, 21, 44, 91, 104, 124
Newton, Sir Isaac ix
Nietzsche 20
Nirvana 120, 121, 130
Notes from Underground (Dostoevsky) xiii
Novalis 120
NP, see *Porphyrii Philosophi Platonici* (Nauck)

Odysseus 2, 61
Odyssey (Homer) 2, 61, 127
Olympia, Olympiad 7, 9, 10, 13, 14, 20,

21, 30, 64, 134, 138, 143
Olympus, Mount, Olympian Gods 18, 62, 111, 121, 130, 133, 135, 144
On Famous Men (Neanthes) 5
On Famous Men (Satyros) 5
On The Making of The World (Hierocles) 3
On Nature (Empedocles) 5, 11, 13, 14, 18, 19, 20, 27, 34, 37, 38, 52, 59, 60, 67, 70, 73, 79, 83, 84, 98, 103, 116, 118, 120, 127, 128, 131, 132, 133, 134, 142, 143, 144, 145
On Osiris and Isis (Plutarch) 5
On Poets (Aristotle) 136
On Providence (Proclus) 4
On Providence (Synesius) 4
On The Pythian Oracle (Plutarch) 5
On The Qualities Of Animate Beings (Aelianos) 3
On The Starting Points Which Lead Us To The Intelligible (Porphyry) 4
On What Philosophers Like (Aëtius) 3
Orphic Mysteries 106, 119, 126, 130
Osiris 5
Ovid xiii

Painters 48, 140, 141
Pantheia 13
Paradox, Paradoxical xii, 25, 32, 34
Parallel Lives of Greek and Roman Statesmen and Generals (Plutarch) 5
Parmenides (and see *Die Fragmente der Vorsokratiker*) 6, 9, 11, 25, 26, 27, 28, 29, 30, 31, 36, 38, 41, 47, 53, 57, 58, 82, 85, 89, 109
Passages 73, 74, 78, 79, 82, 85, 93, 94
Pausanias 11, 16, 19, 20, 21, 54, 88, 104, 133
Peisianax 16
Peleponnese 14
Peleponnesian War 20, 22
Pericles 12, 13, 109

Persephone 21
Pericles (Plutarch) xvii, 109
Persia, Persians 22, 23, 24, 33, 35, 40, 120
PF see *De Fortuna Alexandri* (Plutarch)
Phaeacians 61
Phaedo (Plato) 97
Phaedrus 123
Pherekydes 43, 106, 119
Philolaos 9, 36, 37, 118
Philoponos (John) 3, 70, 87
Philosophy of the Greeks, The (Edward Zeller, ed. Nestle) 125
Phoenicia, Phoenician 4, 23, 40
Pindar 136, 145
Plato, Platonic 4, 5, 6, 10, 21, 23, 25, 26, 27, 33, 35, 37, 43, 46, 82, 89, 97, 100, 123, 124, 125, 127, 141
Plotinus 4
Plutarch 5, 44, 51f, 70, 80, 96, 99, 108, 109, 110, 114
Poe, Edgar Allan ix
Poetica (Aristotle) xvii, 2, 28, 136
Poetry/Poet/Poetic 1, 28, 45, 56, 59, 64, 123, 131, 136, 137, 138, 139, 140, 141, 142, 143, 144, 145
POL see *de facie in orbe lunae* (Plutarch)
Polycrates 35
Porphyrii Philosophi Platonici (A. Nauck) 36
Porphyry 4, 36, 61
Poseidon 59, 60, 120
Pound, Ezra viii, xiv
PP see *Pericles* (Plutarch)
PQC see *Quaestiones Conviviales* (Plutarch)
Pregnancy 74, 94, 95
Proclus 3, 4
Prodicos of Kea 24
Prometheus 100
Protagoras (Plato) 23
Protagoras, the Sophist of Abdera 13, 24

Ptolemy VI 5

Purifications 5, 8, 14, 17, 18, 19, 20, 38, 52, 59, 60, 83, 84, 89, 116, 117, 119, 121, 122, 127, 128, 130, 131, 132, 133, 134, 137, 142, 143, 144, 145

Pythagoras, Pythagorean 3, 4, 9, 11, 14, 15, 19, 23, 35, 36, 37, 38, 41, 42, 43, 58, 63, 67, 79, 84, 90, 97, 98, 101, 104, 109, 118, 119, 120, 126, 130, 133, 142, 143

Quadrivium 3

Quaestiones Conviviales (Plutarch) xvii, 5, 80, 96

Quaestiones Naturales (Plutarch) 5

Quaestiones Romanae (Plutarch) xvii, 108

A Reader's Guide to T. S. Eliot (G. Williamson) xv

Renaissance 24

Respiration (through the skin) 92, 98

Resurrection 12, 19, 34

Revue De Métaphysique et de Morale 56

Rhadamanthus 125

Rhetoric 25, 26

Rhetorica xvii, 2, 28

Rhodes 5, 7, 8, 62

Rolland, Romain 1, 20

Roman, Rome 5, 7, 21, 22, 51f

Sacrifice, Sacrificial Animal, Bloody Sacrifice 15, 16, 37, 61, 63, 64, 66, 122, 123, 125, 129, 131, 142

Samos 22, 35

Satyros 5, 10, 12, 13

Scheria 127

Schopenhauer 120

Scythia, Scythian 23, 126

Sea 29, 31, 53, 90, 91, 98, 112, 122

Selinus 8, 11

Semen 40, 96, 100

Sensation 71, 73, 74, 76, 78, 79, 80, 81, 82, 83, 85, 114

Sex/Sexual Organ 30, 53, 99, 116

Shakespeare, William ix, xiii

Sicily, Sicilian 7, 15, 16, 22, 23, 44, 61, 109, 126

Sikeliot 8

Sikels 61, 62

Simplicius, also see *Doxographi Graeci* 4, 41, 42, 70, 87

Sin 14, 119, 120, 121, 122, 125, 131, 142

Sitzungsberichte Der Berliner Akademie Der Wissenschaften (Wilamowitz) xvii, 9, 127

Socrates, Socratic 3, 11, 21, 23, 25, 27, 30, 43, 97, 115, 124, 125

Solon 23

Sophistici Elenchi (Aristotle) xvii, 2, 12, 25

Sophists 13, 21, 24, 26, 43, 124

Soranos 95

Sosicles 51f

Soul 23, 54, 63, 97, 118, 121, 123, 124, 131, 142

Sparta, Spartan 22, 119

Sphairos vi, xi, xiv, xv, 29, 30, 31, 46, 49, 52, 53, 54, 57, 58, 59, 65, 66, 67, 71, 72, 89, 100, 102, 103, 106, 107, 116, 117, 120, 121, 135, 138, 139, 144

Spinoza 117, 130

Stephanos the Byzantine 5

Stobaeus, Ioannis (C. Wachsmuth) xvii, 47, 70

Stoics 2, 4

Stration 10

Strife vi, x, xi, xii, xiii, 20, 46, 48, 49, 50, 52, 54, 55, 56, 59, 62, 64, 65, 66, 68, 69, 70, 71, 72, 100, 101, 102, 103, 104, 113, 122, 138, 141

Stromateis 4

Suidas 25

Sun 29, 34, 44, 53, 58, 85, 107, 108, 109, 111, 112, 113, 114, 115, 117, 122, 137

Symposium (Plato) 100, 141

Synesius 4

Syracuse, Syracusan 16, 22, 26, 37

Tartarus 124
Telauges 9, 36, 118
Thales 23, 24, 40, 41, 108, 109
Thebes, Theban 23, 36, 97
Themistocles 23
Theocritus xiii
Theogony (Hesiod) 106
Theophrastus, also see *Doxographi Graeci* 6, 42, 61, 75, 76, 77, 78, 79, 90, 96, 98, 107
Theseus 18
Thessaly 26
Thetis 101
Thomson, G. 125
Thousand, The 8, 10, 11, 12, 15
Thrace 5, 21
Thucydides 8, 26
Thurii 13, 14, 34
Timaeus 4, 13, 23
Tradition and the Individual Talent (T. S. Eliot) viii
Transmigration of souls 15, 37, 38, 63, 118, 121, 123, 138, 142
Trees/Bushes 48, 56, 61, 83, 96, 97, 98, 99, 100, 103, 110, 127, 129, 131, 140, 144
Time 27, 32, 41, 85
Triptolemos 101
Trojans 119
Tyre 4

Universe 28, 29, 30, 31, 32, 34, 38, 43, 54, 57, 84, 90, 106, 116, 117, 128, 133, 135
Valery, Paul ix
Van Rooten, Luis d'Antin vii
Varied History 3
VH, see *De Heraclides* (O. Voss)
Voss, O. xvii, 9, 10, 11, 16, 119

Waste Land, The viii, x
Water x, xiii, 31, 40, 41, 42, 45, 50, 51, 59, 68, 77, 92, 93, 94, 100, 102, 108, 111, 136
Welsh 61
Whole, The 27, 46, 68, 69, 74, 117
Wilamowitz xvii, 9, 127
Williamson, George xv
Wind 11, 19, 91, 112, 123
WS, see *Sitzungsberichte Der Berliner Akademie Der Wissenschaften* (Wilamowitz)

Xenophanes, also see *Die Fragmente der Vorsokratiker* 25, 30, 31, 40, 42, 51, 53, 57, 106, 117
Xenophon 75
Xerxes 8

Year's Length 40, 57, 65, 107, 130
Yeats, W. B. viii, ix, xiii

Zeller, Edward 125, 126
Zeno 25, 34
Zeus 18, 44, 59, 60, 120, 129, 137